Sunset

Stir-Fry
COOK BOOK

Recipes in this book were previously published
as part of the *Sunset Complete Wok Cook Book*

By the Editors of

Sunset Books

and Sunset Magazine

Lane Publishing Co. ■ *Menlo Park, California*

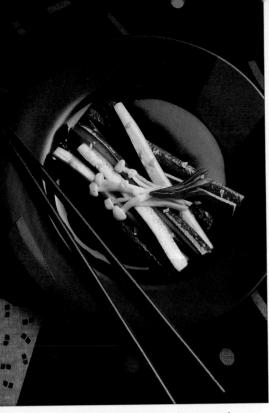

A work of edible art, garlic-seasoned Zucchini Sticks (recipe on page 92) display a garnish of enoki mushrooms and red bell pepper.

Coordinating Editors
Linda J. Selden
Deborah Thomas Kramer

Contributing Editors
Ginger Smith Bate
Sue Brownlee
Rebecca LaBrum
Susan Warton

Design
Joe di Chiarro
Cynthia Hanson

Illustrations
Susan Jaekel

Photo Stylist
JoAnn Masaoka

Food Stylist
Judith A. Gaulke

What Could Be Simpler?

A skillet, a spatula, and a few minutes of your time—these, plus fresh ingredients, are the elements of stir-frying. Understandably, it's a popular technique with time-conscious cooks. But beyond its efficiency, stir-frying also brings out the best of good food. It seals in juices and flavors, along with vitamins and minerals, and it intensifies colors. Vegetables become crisp, meats silken and tender.

Traditionally associated with the cooking of Asia, stir-frying lends itself well to other cuisines too. You'll find recipes in this book for dishes from such diverse cooking arenas as Italy, France, and the American Southwest. Stir-frying can even manage an entire menu—from appetizer to dessert.

For our recipes, we provide a nutritional analysis prepared by Hill Nutrition Associates, Inc., of New York, stating calorie count; grams of protein, carbohydrates, and total fat; and milligrams of cholesterol and sodium. Generally, the nutritional information applies to a single serving, based on the largest number of servings given for each recipe.

The nutritional analysis does not include optional ingredients or those for which no specific amount is stated. If an ingredient is listed with an option, the information was calculated using the first choice. Likewise, if a range is given for the amount of an ingredient, values were figured based on the first, lower amount.

For their valuable editorial assistance, we extend special thanks to Tori Bunting and Mary Jane Swanson. We also thank The Abacus and Crate & Barrel for their generosity in sharing props for use in our photographs.

About the Recipes

All of the recipes in this book were tested and developed in the *Sunset* test kitchens.

Home Economics Editor, Sunset Magazine
Jerry Anne Di Vecchio

Photographers: Victor Budnik, 47, 79; Darrow Watt, 7, 63; Tom Wyatt, 39, 42, 55, 58; Nikolay Zurek, 2, 10, 15, 18, 23, 26, 31, 34, 50, 66, 71, 74, 82, 87, 90, 95.

Cover: Tantalizing color and fresh, crisp vegetables characterize stir-fried Tomato Beef (recipe on page 19), a Cantonese specialty. Design by Williams & Ziller Design. Photography by Victor Budnik. Photo styling by JoAnn Masaoka. Food styling by Judith A. Gaulke.

Editor, Sunset Books: Elizabeth L. Hogan

Third printing November 1989

Contents

Special Features

Stir-frying

Simplicity itself, stir-frying is the art of quickly tossing and stirring together bite-size morsels of food in a little oil over high heat. In minutes, you'll be rewarded with a dish that's extraordinarily rich in flavor, color, and texture. Stir-frying simply and naturally brings out the best in food.

With this book, you can sample exquisite dishes from cuisines around the world. In fact, you can prepare an entire meal—from appetizer through dessert—with a minimum of fuss and a maximum of fun, simply by stir-frying. All you need are a skillet or a wok, a spatula, and a little time. Though chopping ingredients takes some time, stir-frying itself is no more than a flash in the pan.

Getting equipped

If you don't already own a good skillet, you may want to purchase one especially for stir-frying. Or you can stir-fry in a wok in the Oriental tradition.

Skillets—your options. Look for a l0- to l4-inch skillet that responds quickly to temperature change. Pans are available in a variety of materials.

Cast or heavy-gauge iron skillets evenly distribute and retain heat, but they're heavy and prone to rust. *Aluminum pans* conduct heat well; they're also conveniently lightweight and relatively inexpensive. But aluminum can react with certain foods in a way that causes slight changes in flavor and color. *Stainless steel pans* are lightweight and easy to maintain, but they may conduct heat unevenly. *Porcelain* bonded to metal will not react with foods and is easy to clean. But these pans may not brown food well.

Copper pans conduct heat better than the others, but they're usually quite expensive. To keep their beauty, copper pans must be polished after every use. Because copper reacts with all foods, the pans are always lined, usually with tin. This lining eventually needs replacing.

Special pan treatments can improve on pans that otherwise might not make good choices for stir-frying. For example, a layer of aluminum added to a stainless steel pan will make it a better heat conductor. Aluminum pans are sometimes finished with a nonstick, nonreactive surface.

Woks—for traditional stir-frying. Thanks to its unique shape, the wok is the model of stir-frying efficiency, as well as its original inspiration. The wok's sloping sides and rounded bottom heat up fast and evenly, providing an optimal surface for cooking.

Most traditional woks are made from heavy-gauge rolled carbon steel, which conducts heat beautifully. These woks require seasoning before use and careful maintenance afterwards. Before using a new carbon steel wok, wash it with soapy water. Rinse it well and then dry it directly over medium heat on your range until no moisture remains. Next, rub the inside with a paper towel dampened with 2 teaspoons of salad oil. Wipe off any excess oil. After each use, wash the wok with soapy water, using a soft brush to scrub off any food that sticks. Rinse the wok well and dry it on the range. If the wok isn't kept completely dry between uses, it will rust.

Aluminum and stainless steel woks are also available. They need no seasoning and won't rust, so you can simply clean them as you would any other aluminum or stainless pan. Though both types are good conductors, neither will distribute heat as evenly as a carbon steel wok.

Electric woks are tops for tabletop cooking. When you're entertaining, you can cook and present your stir-fry at the table while your guests observe or actively participate. But some electric woks are less responsive to heat than conventional woks, so they may not work as efficiently for stir-frying.

Accessories. While a good skillet or wok takes center stage for stir-frying's dramatic action, just as important are two stagehands: a spatula to keep things moving and a lid to simmer them down. If you're using a frying pan, be sure your model comes with a lid. Choose a spatula to suit your choice of pan. For a wok, the typical spatula has a long, wood-tipped handle and a wide, curved edge.

Step-by-step stir-frying

Stir-frying is easy to master. The tricky part is learning to work with higher than usual cooking heat.

Both hands come into play—and dexterity improves with practice. You use one to hold the pan, moving it on and off the heat source as needed to control temperature. At the same time, you use the other hand to stir, keeping ingredients moving. Foods cook amazingly quickly this way.

For a look at stir-frying in action, along with step-by-step directions, see pages 6 and 7.

Preparation. The first—and most important—rule of stir-frying is to have everything ready to go before you start cooking. There's no time for chopping ingredients or for making a cooking sauce once the pan is hot. Action is almost instantaneous.

First, you'll need to cut up the ingredients you're using (see the drawings below). Be sure to cut pieces as uniform as possible in size and shape. This uniformity is especially important in stir-frying, since the food is cooked so quickly; if you stir-fry food that's cut unevenly, the result will also be uneven—ranging from almost raw to overdone.

For meats and certain fibrous vegetables, cutting slanting or diagonal slices serves two purposes: it helps to tenderize the food as well as exposes the most surface possible to the pan's heat. If a recipe asks for thinly sliced ingredients, simply cut straight down rather than at a slant. Julienne strips should be about the size of a wooden matchstick. Dice means cutting into ⅛- to ¼-inch cubes.

Basic techniques. Place all your ingredients and any cooking sauce within easy reach. Set the clean, dry pan over high heat (or as the recipe directs). When the pan is hot, add oil as specified in the recipe (ours usually call for salad oil, because it can withstand high temperatures without burning). When the oil is hot, it's ready for stir-frying. If the recipe specifies butter, reduce the heat to medium-high or lower; otherwise, the butter may burn.

Add ingredients as the recipe directs. Quickly stir and toss, keeping the food in motion. If the recipe directs you to add oil at any point, bring it to rippling-hot before adding more food to the pan. If you're stir-frying firm vegetables, you may need to add water and cover the pan for a few minutes to steam them tender; let your recipe guide you on this.

Braising—one step further

Braising, a technique closely related to stir-frying, appears in a few recipes in this book. You follow the standard procedure of browning meat and briefly cooking vegetables in hot oil. Then you add liquid, cover the pan, and simmer over low heat until ingredients are tender. To braise in a round-bottomed wok, you'll need to set the wok in a ring stand to keep it stable.

Reducing sodium in stir-fry recipes

Because Oriental cuisines offer a myriad of tempting stir-fry applications, many of our recipes showcase the foods and seasonings of Asia. If you often use Oriental-style recipes, you may be consuming more sodium than you want.

Fortunately, it's a simple matter to reduce the sodium content of most dishes. Obviously, you can just cut down or eliminate salt from the recipe. Another method is to use reduced-sodium soy sauce. Or you can substitute homemade, unsalted chicken broth (recipe on page 53) or canned low-sodium chicken broth for the regular canned or reconstituted type. Another way around sodium is to cut down on serving sizes, then round out the meal with generous portions of plain rice or noodles.

To diagonally slice fibrous vegetables, such as celery, cut crosswise on the diagonal into ⅛- to ¼-inch-thick slanting slices.

To slice meat, such as flank steak, cut while partially frozen, across the grain, at a 45° angle.

To thinly slice food, such as mushrooms, cut straight down at a right angle.

To julienne, cut food, such as zucchini, into 2- to 3-inch lengths; then slice lengthwise ⅛ inch thick. Stack 2 or 3 slices and cut into ⅛-inch strips.

To dice food, such as potatoes, cut as directed for julienne strips, then cut crosswise into small squares. For larger dice, start with thicker strips.

How to stir-fry

When you stir-fry, you don't really fry; you cook foods quickly by stirring and tossing them in a small amount of hot fat. This kind of flash-cooking seals in juices and keeps flavors fresh; it's a technique you can use to make dishes of every kind, from appetizers to desserts All stir-fry recipes follow the same basic steps; once you've mastered the method, you can easily create recipes of your own.

In addition to your skillet or wok, the only tool you need for successful stir-frying is a long-handled spatula with a wide, curved edge. You'll also need to keep these points in mind:

- Do all your cutting in advance. Foods should be cut in small, uniform pieces or thin slices.

- Prepare any seasonings and sauce mixtures in advance. Once you start to cook, you won't have time to stop and create a sauce.

- Assemble the cut-up meat and/or vegetables, seasonings, sauce mixture, and salad oil or other fat near the range.

- Place a clean, dry pan over the heat specified in the recipe—typically high heat, sometimes medium or medium-high. When the pan is hot, add the fat as directed. Heat oil until it's hot enough to ripple when the pan is tilted from side to side; heat butter until it's foamy.

- Add any seasonings (garlic or ginger, for example). Holding the pan handle in one hand and a wide spatula in the other, stir and toss the seasonings until lightly browned.

     Now add meat, if used. (Never add more than about 1 pound at a time; if you have more, cook it in batches.) Spread the pieces evenly over the pan's surface; stir and toss until lightly browned all over. Turn meat out of pan.

- Add 1 to 2 tablespoons more oil (or other fat). When oil is hot, add vegetables, one variety at a time. Start with the type that has the longest cooking time (see page 8); stir-fry just until tender-crisp to bite, lifting and tossing vegetables to coat them with oil. Turn out of pan; repeat to cook remaining vegetables. (Or simply add all vegetables in sequence, timing your additions so all will be done at the same time.) For dense or fibrous vegetables such as broccoli or asparagus, you may need to add a little water, then cover the pan and steam the vegetable slightly, stirring often.

- Return meat and vegetables to pan. Stir cooking sauce to reblend cornstarch; pour into pan. Stir until sauce boils and thickens. Serve.

NOTE: Use the cooking times given in our recipes as guides, not absolutes. Actual cooking time will vary, depending upon the kind of pan you use and the intensity of the heat source.

(Pictured on facing page)

Chinese Chicken & Zucchini

Preparation time: About 20 minutes, plus 30 minutes to soak mushrooms

Marinating time: 15 minutes

Cooking time: About 10 minutes

Follow the step-by-step photos on the facing page to make this classic stir-fry of crisp vegetable chunks and spicy chicken.

> 5 dried Oriental mushrooms
> 2 teaspoons *each* soy sauce, cornstarch, dry sherry, and water
> Dash of white pepper
> 1 clove garlic, minced
> ½ teaspoon minced fresh ginger
> 2 teaspoons fermented salted black beans, rinsed, drained, and finely chopped
> 1½ pounds chicken breasts, skinned and boned
> 3½ tablespoons salad oil
> Cooking Sauce (recipe at left on page 38)
> ½ pound zucchini
> 1 whole bamboo shoot, cut into small pieces, or ½ cup sliced bamboo shoots
> 1 red or green bell pepper, seeded and cut into 1-inch squares

Soak mushrooms in warm water to cover for 30 minutes, then drain. Cut off and discard stems; squeeze caps dry, thinly slice, and set aside.

In a bowl, mix soy, cornstarch, sherry, water, pepper, garlic, ginger, and beans. Cut chicken into bite-size pieces; add to marinade and stir to coat, then stir in 1½ teaspoons of the oil. Let marinate for 15 minutes. Meanwhile, prepare Cooking Sauce; set aside. Roll-cut zucchini as shown on facing page.

Place a wok over high heat. When pan is hot, add 2 tablespoons of the oil. When oil is hot, add chicken mixture and stir-fry until meat is no longer pink in center; cut to test (about 3 minutes). Remove from pan and set aside.

Pour remaining 1 tablespoon oil into pan. When oil is hot, add mushrooms, bamboo shoots, zucchini, and bell pepper. Stir-fry for 1 minute, then add 2 tablespoons water, cover, and cook until zucchini and bell pepper are tender-crisp to bite (about 3 more minutes). Return chicken to pan. Stir Cooking Sauce, pour into pan, and stir until sauce boils and thickens. Makes 3 or 4 servings.

Per serving: 296 calories, 29 g protein, 12 g carbohydrates, 15 g total fat, 65 mg cholesterol, 836 mg sodium

Stir-frying Chinese Chicken & Zucchini (Recipe on facing page)

1 Soak dried mushrooms in warm water for 30 minutes. Cut off and discard hard stems; cut caps into ¼-inch-thick slices.

2 Cut boned chicken breasts into bite-size pieces. Then add chicken to soy marinade flavored with garlic, ginger, and fermented black beans; stir to coat and let marinate for 15 minutes.

3 Roll-cut zucchini by making a diagonal slice straight down through squash, giving it a quarter turn, and slicing again. Cut pepper into 1-inch squares; cut bamboo shoot into small pieces.

4 When vegetables are tender-crisp, return cooked chicken to pan and toss to heat through.

5 Add cooking sauce, pouring it in around edges of pan so it will heat quickly. Cook, stirring constantly, until sauce thickens (about 30 seconds).

6 Stir-fried vegetables have bright color, crisp texture; chicken morsels are tender and juicy. To serve the meal Chinese style, provide each diner with an individual bowl of rice.

Stir-frying Fresh Vegetables

Perfect stir-fried vegetables are bright, colorful, and naturally sweet in flavor, with a texture that's crisp yet tender to the bite. They're quick to fix, too—most types cook in 5 minutes or less.

To stir-fry:

1) Cut vegetables into slices or small pieces, as directed in chart below.

2) Place wok over high heat. When wok is hot, add specified amount of oil; when oil is hot, add vegetables all at once and stir-fry, uncovered, for time noted in chart.

3) Add designated amount of liquid (regular-strength chicken or beef broth or water); cover and cook for remaining time. As vegetables cook, all or most of liquid will evaporate; because there's no cooking liquid to drain off and discard, vitamins and minerals are retained.

Remember that the times noted below should be used as guides. Actual times will vary, depending on the freshness and maturity of the vegetables and on individual preference. Taste after the minimum cooking time; if you prefer a softer texture, continue cooking, tasting often, until vegetables are done to your liking.

If you'd like to cook a medley of several vegetables, add the firmest kind to the wok first; cook for the time indicated, adding the more tender vegetables near the end of the cooking time. Or cook each vegetable separately, then combine them all for reheating and blending of flavors.

A final pointer for success: never crowd the wok. Cook no more than 5 cups of cut-up vegetables in a 12- to 14-inch wok. To prepare more servings than you can cook at once, just cut up the total quantity of vegetables you'll need, then cook them in two or more batches. Stir-frying is so fast that you can keep the first portions warm, without flavor loss, while the others cook.

Vegetable *4 to 5 cups cut-up vegetable*	Tablespoons salad oil	Minutes to stir-fry uncovered	Tablespoons broth or water	Minutes to cook covered
Asparagus. Cut into ½-inch slanting slices	1	1	1–2	2–3
Beans, green, Italian, wax. Cut into 1-inch pieces	1	1	4	4–7
Bok choy. See Swiss chard				
Broccoli. Cut into ¼-inch slices	1	1	3–5	3–5
Cabbage, green, red, Savoy. Shredded	1	1	2	3–4
Cabbage, napa. Cut white part into 1-inch slices; shred leaves and add during last 2–3 minutes of cooking time	1	1–2	2	4–5
Carrots. Cut into ¼-inch slices	1	1	2–3	3–5
Cauliflower. Flowerets, cut into ¼-inch slices	1	1	3–4	4–5
Celery. Cut into ¼-inch slices	1	1	1–2	1–3
Fennel. Cut into ¼-inch slices	1	2–3	No liquid necessary	Not necessary
Leeks, white part only. Cut into ¼-inch slices	1	1	3–4	3
Mushrooms. Cut into ¼-inch slices	1	3–4	No liquid necessary	Not necessary
Onions, dry. Cut into ¼-inch slices	1	1	No liquid necessary	3–4
Parsnips. Cut into ¼-inch slices	2	1	6–8	4–6
Pea pods, Chinese.	1	3	1	½
Peas, green. Shelled	1	1	3–4	2–3
Peppers, green or red bell. Cut into 1-inch pieces	1	1	2–3	3–5
Rutabagas. Cut into ¼-inch slices	1	1	4–5	5–6
Spinach. Leaves, whole or coarsely chopped	1	½	No liquid necessary	2–3
Sprouts, bean.	1	1	1	½–1½
Squash, summer (crookneck, pattypan, zucchini). Cut into ¼-inch slices	1	1	2–4	3–4
Swiss chard. Cut stems into ¼-inch slices; shred leaves and add during last 2–3 minutes of cooking time	1	1	1	3½–4½
Turnips. Cut into ¼-inch slices	1	1	4–5	4–5

Appetizers

Meatballs with Ginger Glaze

Preparation time: About 25 minutes

Cooking time: About 45 minutes (about 10 minutes/batch)

A sweet and sour sauce that's nippy with fresh ginger coats these small meatballs. If you prepare the dish in an electric wok, you can serve it right in the cooking pan.

> Ginger Glaze (recipe follows)
> 1 can (about 8 oz.) water chestnuts, drained and finely chopped
> 1 cup chopped green onions (including tops)
> 2 pounds lean ground pork
> 2 tablespoons soy sauce
> 2 eggs
> ¾ cup fine dry bread crumbs
> About 1 tablespoon salad oil

Prepare Ginger Glaze; set aside.

In a bowl, combine water chestnuts, onions, pork, soy, eggs, and bread crumbs. Mix thoroughly with a fork or your hands, then shape mixture into ¾-inch balls (you should have about 72).

Place a wok over medium-high heat; when wok is hot, add 1 tablespoon of the oil. When oil is hot, add 24 meatballs and stir-fry until well browned (about 10 minutes). Remove from wok and set aside. Repeat to brown remaining meatballs, adding more oil as needed. Clean wok.

Place wok over high heat; when wok is hot, pour in Ginger Glaze and stir until glaze boils vigorously. Add meatballs and simmer for about 10 minutes. If using an electric wok, serve in wok; otherwise, transfer to a chafing dish. Provide wooden picks for spearing meatballs. Makes about 6 dozen meatballs (10 to 12 servings).

Ginger Glaze. In a large bowl, smoothly blend ½ cup **water** and ¼ cup **cornstarch.** Add 1 cup *each* **unsweetened pineapple juice** and **regular-strength beef broth,** ½ cup **cider vinegar,** ⅓ cup **sugar,** 1 tablespoon **soy sauce,** and 2 tablespoons minced **fresh ginger.**

Per serving: 233 calories, 17 g protein, 19 g carbohydrates, 9 g total fat, 97 mg cholesterol, 447 mg sodium

Quick Pot Stickers

Preparation time: About 1 hour

Cooking time: About 1 hour (about 15 minutes/batch)

Traditional pot stickers (page 11) are delicious, but they do take time to make. It isn't hard to speed up the preparation, though—instead of using home-made wrappers, just start with the purchased ones (*gyoza*) sold in some grocery stores and Asian markets.

> 2 small whole chicken breasts (about ¾ lb. *each*), skinned, boned, and split
> ¼ cup sesame oil
> 1 cup finely chopped celery
> ½ cup chopped green onions (including tops)
> 3 tablespoons dry sherry
> 2 tablespoons cornstarch
> 1 teaspoon sugar
> ½ teaspoon salt
> 1 package (14 oz.) pot sticker wrappers (*gyoza*) or won ton skins
> ¼ cup salad oil
> 1 cup water
> Rice wine vinegar, soy sauce, and chili oil

Rinse chicken and pat dry, then chop finely. Place in a bowl and stir in sesame oil, celery, onions, sherry, cornstarch, sugar, and salt.

Set out 6 to 8 wrappers at a time; keep remaining wrappers tightly covered. Mound 2 teaspoons of the filling on each wrapper. To shape each pot sticker, fold dough in half over filling. Pinch about ½ inch of curved edge closed; continue to pinch closed, forming 3 tucks along dough edge, until entire curve is sealed. Set pot sticker down firmly, seam side up, so it will sit flat. Cover lightly until all pot stickers are shaped. (At this point, you may freeze pot stickers as directed on page 11. Cook without thawing as directed below.)

Place a wok over medium heat; when wok is hot, add 1 tablespoon of the salad oil. When oil is hot, add 12 pot stickers, seam side up. Cook until bottoms are golden brown (5 to 7 minutes). Pour in ¼ cup of the water; reduce heat to low, cover, and cook until liquid is absorbed (6 to 10 more minutes). Remove from wok and keep warm. Repeat to cook remaining pot stickers, using remaining salad oil and water.

Offer pot stickers with vinegar, soy, and chili oil on the side for dipping. Makes about 4 dozen pot stickers (about 10 servings).

Per serving: 273 calories, 14 g protein, 24 g carbohydrates, 13 g total fat, 54 mg cholesterol, 151 mg sodium

---

Note: Recipes may be prepared in either a skillet or a wok.

Golden brown Pot Stickers (recipe on facing page) are an
ever-popular appetizer, first course, or light entrée. Let guests dip these
dumplings into soy, vinegar, and chili oil, combined or served in
individual bowls.

(Pictured on facing page)

Pot Stickers

Preparation time: About 1½ hours, plus 30 minutes to let dough rest

Cooking time: About 1¾ hours (about 25 minutes/batch)

These savory filled dumplings—called *guotie* in Chinese—make a tasty and substantial first course for parties or everyday meals. They freeze well, so you can make them well in advance.

> Shrimp Filling (recipe follows)
> 3 cups all-purpose flour
> ¼ teaspoon salt
> 1 cup boiling water
> ¼ cup salad oil
> About 1⅓ cups regular-strength chicken broth
> Soy sauce, rice wine vinegar, and chili oil

Prepare filling; cover and refrigerate.

In a bowl, combine flour and salt; mix in water until dough is evenly moistened and begins to hold together. On a lightly floured board, knead dough until very smooth and satiny (about 5 minutes). Cover and let rest at room temperature for 30 minutes.

Divide dough into 2 equal portions. Keep 1 portion covered; roll out other portion about ⅛ inch thick (or thinner). Cut dough into 3½- to 4-inch circles with a round cookie cutter or a clean, empty can with both ends removed. Repeat with scraps and remaining dough.

Mound 2 teaspoons of the filling on each circle. To shape each pot sticker, fold dough in half over filling. Pinch about ½ inch of curved edge closed; continue to pinch closed, forming 3 tucks along dough edge, until entire curve is sealed. Set pot sticker down firmly, seam side up, so it will sit flat. Cover lightly until all pot stickers are shaped. (At this point, you may place pot stickers in a single layer on a baking sheet and freeze until hard, then transfer to a heavy plastic bag, seal, and return to freezer for up to 1 month. Cook without thawing as directed below.)

Place a wok over medium heat; when wok is hot, add 1 tablespoon of the salad oil. When oil is hot, add 12 pot stickers, seam side up. Cook until bottoms are golden brown (8 to 10 minutes). Pour in ⅓ cup of the broth and immediately cover wok tightly. Reduce heat to low and cook for 10 minutes (15 minutes if frozen). Uncover and continue to cook until all liquid is absorbed. Remove from wok and keep warm. Repeat to cook remaining pot stickers, using remaining salad oil and broth.

Offer pot stickers with soy, vinegar, and chili oil on the side for dipping. Makes about 4 dozen pot stickers (about 10 servings).

Shrimp Filling. Shell, devein, and finely chop ½ pound **medium-size raw shrimp.** Combine shrimp with ½ pound **lean ground pork,** 1 cup finely shredded **cabbage,** ¼ cup minced **green onions** (including tops), ¼ cup chopped **mushrooms,** 1 clove **garlic** (minced or pressed), ½ teaspoon **salt,** and 2 tablespoons **oyster sauce** or soy sauce. Mix well.

Per serving: 253 calories, 13 g protein, 30 g carbohydrates, 9 g total fat, 42 mg cholesterol, 497 mg sodium

Beef Chiang Mai

Preparation time: About 10 minutes

Cooking time: About 15 minutes

Warm, spicy beef wrapped in cool lettuce leaves makes a tempting appetizer; the dish is traditional in northern Thailand. If you like, you can wash and crisp the lettuce leaves a day ahead.

> ¼ cup short-grain rice (such as pearl) or long-grain rice
> 1 pound lean ground beef
> 1 teaspoon *each* sugar and crushed red pepper
> ½ cup *each* thinly sliced green onions (including tops) and chopped fresh mint
> 2 tablespoons chopped fresh cilantro (coriander)
> ¼ cup lemon juice
> 1½ tablespoons soy sauce
> Small inner leaves from 2 large or 3 small heads butter lettuce
> About 36 fresh mint sprigs

Place a wok over medium heat. When wok is hot, add rice and stir-fry until golden (about 5 minutes). Remove from heat and transfer to a blender or food processor; whirl until finely ground. Set aside.

Return wok to medium heat; when wok is hot, crumble in beef and cook, stirring, just until meat begins to lose its pinkness (about 3 minutes). Add ground rice, sugar, red pepper, onions, chopped mint, cilantro, lemon juice, and soy; stir until well combined. Pour into a serving dish and surround with lettuce leaves and mint sprigs.

To eat, spoon beef mixture onto lettuce leaves, top with a mint sprig, roll up, and eat out of hand. Makes about 12 servings.

Per serving: 123 calories, 7 g protein, 5 g carbohydrates, 8 g total fat, 28 mg cholesterol, 157 mg sodium

Note: Recipes may be prepared in either a skillet or a wok.

Ginger Chicken Wings

Preparation time: About 15 minutes

Cooking time: About 25 minutes

Like the ginger-glazed meatballs on page 9, these hearty chicken wings feature a snappy fresh-ginger sauce. Serve them hot or at room temperature.

> Cooking Sauce (recipe follows)
> 12 chicken wings (about 2¼ lbs. *total*)
> 5 tablespoons salad oil
> 2 tablespoons *each* soy sauce and minced fresh ginger
> 2 teaspoons *each* cornstarch and sugar
> ¼ cup regular-strength chicken broth
> ⅓ cup sliced green onions (including tops), optional

Prepare Cooking Sauce; set aside.

Cut off and discard tips of chicken wings, then cut wing sections apart at the joint. Rinse and pat dry.

In a bowl, stir together 2 tablespoons of the oil, soy, ginger, cornstarch, and sugar. Add chicken pieces; stir to coat.

Place a wok over high heat; when wok is hot, add remaining 3 tablespoons oil. When oil is hot, add chicken mixture and cook, uncovered, stirring occasionally, until chicken is browned (about 5 minutes). Stir in broth. Reduce heat to medium, cover, and cook until chicken pulls easily from bone (15 to 20 minutes).

Stir Cooking Sauce, then add to chicken wings. Cook, stirring, until sauce boils and thickens. If made ahead, let cool, then cover and refrigerate for up to 3 days.

Serve chicken wings hot or at room temperature. To serve, arrange wings on a dish; sprinkle with onions, if desired. Makes 4 to 6 servings.

Cooking Sauce. Stir together ¼ cup **regular-strength chicken broth,** 2 teaspoons **cornstarch,** and 2 tablespoons *each* **oyster sauce** and **dry sherry.**

Per serving: 335 calories, 18 g protein, 6 g carbohydrates, 26 g total fat, 71 mg cholesterol, 733 mg sodium

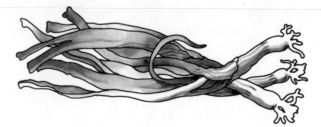

Tequila-Lime Ice with Shrimp

Preparation time: About 45 minutes

Freezing time: 4 to 6 hours

Cooking time: About 5 minutes

A refreshingly tart, super-simple ice perfectly sets off the sweetness of stir-fried shrimp. Make the ice early in the day (or up to a month ahead); cook the shrimp just 30 minutes in advance.

> 1½ teaspoons grated lime peel
> 1 cup sugar
> 2 cups lime juice (about 14 fresh limes; or use bottled juice)
> ½ cup tequila
> 1 cup water
> Stir-fried Shrimp (recipe follows)
> Lime peel strips (optional)

In a 9- by 13-inch pan, stir together grated lime peel, sugar, lime juice, tequila, and water until sugar is dissolved; cover. Freeze until firm (4 to 6 hours) or for up to 1 month.

About 30 minutes before serving, prepare shrimp and set aside; also place 5 to 8 small bowls in the freezer.

With a heavy spoon, break lime ice into chunks. Whirl in a food processor or beat with an electric mixer until a thick, icy slush forms. Immediately spoon into chilled bowls; garnish with strips of lime peel, if desired. Accompany with shrimp. Makes 4 cups ice (5 to 8 first-course servings).

Stir-fried Shrimp. Shell and devein 1 pound **large raw shrimp.** Place a wok over high heat; when wok is hot, add 2 tablespoons **salad oil.** When oil is hot, add shrimp and stir-fry until pink (about 3 minutes). Stir in 2 tablespoons **tequila;** carefully ignite with a match (not beneath an exhaust fan or near flammable items) and shake wok until flames die down. Add 2 tablespoons **lime juice.** Serve at room temperature.

Per serving: 226 calories, 10 g protein, 31 g carbohydrates, 4 g total fat, 65 mg cholesterol, 97 mg sodium

Crunchy Indian Snack

Preparation time: About 10 minutes

Cooking time: About 30 minutes

Spicy Bombay *chiura*, a crunchy Indian snack, is a mixture of legumes, nuts, sesame seeds, and sweet raisins. Serve it in a bowl, as finger food.

¼ cup *each* uncooked lentils, long-grain rice, and dried split peas
3 cups water
2 tablespoons salad oil
1 tablespoon sesame seeds
1 teaspoon *each* ground coriander and ground cumin
½ teaspoon ground turmeric
½ cup *each* salted roasted peanuts and cashews
¼ cup raisins
⅛ to ¼ teaspoon ground red pepper (cayenne)
¼ teaspoon ground cloves
1 teaspoon salt

Rinse lentils, rice, and peas; drain well. Place in a 2- to 3-quart pan and add 3 cups water; bring to a boil over high heat. Boil for 1 minute; then remove from heat, cover, and set aside for 10 minutes. Drain, rinse under cold water, and drain again; spread on paper towels and pat dry.

Place a wok over medium-high heat; when wok is hot, add oil. When oil is hot, add lentils, rice, peas, sesame seeds, coriander, cumin, and turmeric. Cook, stirring, until mixture is toasted (5 to 10 minutes). Remove from heat and stir in peanuts, cashews, raisins, red pepper, cloves, and salt. Let cool. If made ahead, store airtight for up to 1 week. Makes 2 cups.

Per ¼ cup: 215 calories, 7 g protein, 20 g carbohydrates, 13 g total fat, 0 mg cholesterol, 371 mg sodium

Cold Spiced Cabbage

Preparation time: About 10 minutes

Cooking time: 3 minutes

Chilling time: About 4 hours

Garlic, sesame, and crushed red pepper season this simple cold relish. It's a fine addition to an appetizer tray as well as a good complement for a richly seasoned main course.

1 small head napa cabbage (about 1½ lbs.)
2 tablespoons salad oil
2 cloves garlic, minced
⅓ cup water
3 tablespoons *each* sugar and white wine vinegar
½ teaspoon salt
1½ teaspoons sesame oil
¼ to ½ teaspoon crushed red pepper

Cut cabbage into 2-inch pieces. Place a wok over high heat. When wok is hot, add salad oil. When oil begins to heat, add garlic and stir once. Then add cabbage and stir-fry for 30 seconds. Add water, cover, and cook, stirring occasionally, until cabbage is just barely wilted (about 1½ minutes). Remove from heat and pour off any excess liquid. Stir sugar, vinegar, salt, sesame oil, and red pepper into cabbage. Let cool, then cover and refrigerate until cold (about 4 hours) or for up to 1 week. Serve cold. Makes about 2½ cups.

Per ¼ cup: 57 calories, .85 g protein, 6 g carbohydrates, 4 g total fat, 0 mg cholesterol, 116 mg sodium

Spiced Pecans

Preparation time: About 5 minutes

Cooking time: About 3 minutes

Pecans, a favorite in the South, are sautéed in a pungent spice mixture in this Creole-style snack. Your guests will find them hard to resist!

½ teaspoon *each* salt, paprika, and ground red pepper (cayenne)
1 teaspoon white pepper
1 tablespoon fresh or dry rosemary
2 tablespoons butter or margarine
1 tablespoon olive oil
10 ounces (about 2½ cups) pecan halves
1 tablespoon Worcestershire
½ teaspoon liquid hot pepper seasoning

Combine salt, paprika, red pepper, white pepper, and rosemary. Set aside.

Place a wok over high heat; when wok is hot, add butter and oil. When butter is melted, add pecans and stir-fry until nuts are well coated with butter and oil and slightly darker in color (about 1 minute). Add Worcestershire, hot pepper seasoning, and spice mixture; continue to stir-fry until pecans are deep brown (about 1½ more minutes; be careful not to scorch nuts). Let cool. If made ahead, store airtight for up to 2 days. Makes 2½ cups.

Per ¼ cup: 225 calories, 2 g protein, 6 g carbohydrates, 23 g total fat, 6 mg cholesterol, 156 mg sodium

---

Note: Recipes may be prepared in either a skillet or a wok.

Beef, Pork, Veal & Lamb

(Pictured on facing page)

Szechwan Beef

Preparation time: About 10 minutes

Cooking time: About 10 minutes

Tender beef, crisp carrots, and a handful of hot chiles go into this stir-fry. Use small dried chiles or larger ones, as you prefer.

> Cooking Sauce (recipe follows)
> 1 pound lean boneless beef steak (such as top round, flank, or sirloin)
> 2 tablespoons salad oil
> 16 dried hot red chiles
> 2 large carrots, cut into about 3-inch-long julienne strips
> 1 can (about 8 oz.) sliced bamboo shoots, drained (and thinly sliced, if desired)
> Fresh cilantro (coriander) leaves (optional)

Prepare Cooking Sauce and set aside.

Cut beef with the grain into 1½-inch-wide strips; then cut each strip across the grain into ⅛-inch-thick slanting slices. Set aside.

Place a wok over high heat; when wok is hot, add oil. When oil is hot, add chiles and cook, stirring, until chiles just begin to char. Remove chiles from wok; set aside.

Add beef to wok and stir-fry until browned (1½ to 2 minutes); remove from wok and set aside. Add carrots to wok and stir-fry until tender-crisp to bite (about 3 minutes). Add bamboo shoots and stir-fry for 1 more minute.

Return meat and chiles to wok; stir Cooking Sauce and add. Stir until sauce boils and thickens. Garnish with cilantro, if desired. Makes 4 servings.

Cooking Sauce. Stir together 2 tablespoons **soy sauce**, 1 tablespoon **dry sherry**, 2 teaspoons **sugar**, and ½ teaspoon **cornstarch.**

Per serving: 349 calories, 31 g protein, 26 g carbohydrates, 17 g total fat, 65 mg cholesterol, 602 mg sodium

Beef with Napa Cabbage

Preparation time: About 15 minutes

Marinating time: 10 minutes

Cooking time: About 8 minutes

Red bell pepper and green napa cabbage give this entrée its bright, fresh look and flavor. Napa cabbage is sold in most supermarkets; sometimes called Chinese or celery cabbage, it has a sweeter taste and a more tender texture than the familiar head cabbage.

> ½ to ¾ pound lean boneless beef steak (such as top round, flank, or sirloin)
> 1 teaspoon cornstarch
> 1 tablespoon soy sauce
> ½ teaspoon minced fresh ginger
> Cooking Sauce (recipe follows)
> About ¾ pound napa cabbage (about ½ small head)
> ¼ cup salad oil
> 1 clove garlic, minced or pressed
> 1 red bell pepper, seeded and cut into 1-inch squares
> 2 green onions (including tops), thinly sliced

Cut beef with the grain into 1½-inch-wide strips; then cut each strip across the grain into ⅛-inch-thick slanting slices. In a bowl, stir together cornstarch, soy, and ginger. Add beef and stir to coat well. Let marinate for 10 minutes.

Meanwhile, prepare Cooking Sauce and set aside. Also cut cabbage crosswise into ¾-inch slices.

Place a wok over high heat. When wok is hot, add 2 tablespoons of the oil. When oil is hot, add meat mixture. Stir-fry until meat is browned (1½ to 2 minutes); set aside.

Add remaining 2 tablespoons oil to wok. When oil is hot, add garlic and bell pepper. Stir-fry for about 30 seconds. Add cabbage and stir-fry until cabbage is bright green and tender-crisp to bite (about 2 minutes).

Return meat mixture to wok. Stir Cooking Sauce and add, then stir until sauce boils and thickens. Mix in onions. Makes 2 or 3 servings.

Cooking Sauce. Stir together 1 tablespoon *each* **cornstarch** and **sugar**, ½ cup **regular-strength beef broth**, and 1 tablespoon *each* **soy sauce** and **dry sherry.**

Per serving: 386 calories, 29 g protein, 14 g carbohydrates, 23 g total fat, 65 mg cholesterol, 912 mg sodium

Note: Recipes may be prepared in either a skillet or a wok.

Hot chiles, characteristic of Szechwan province, boldly accent
lean, tender strips of sirloin in Szechwan Beef (recipe on facing page).
Slender carrot ribbons and sliced bamboo shoots contribute
color and crispness.

Beef with Bok Choy

Preparation time: About 10 minutes

Marinating time: 15 minutes

Cooking time: About 12 minutes

Crisp bok choy and sweet sesame seeds complement strips of steak in this simple entrée. As you prepare the bok choy, remember to keep stems and leaves separate—they go into the wok at different times.

    Cooking Sauce (recipe follows)
 ¾ pound lean boneless beef steak (such as top round, flank, or sirloin)
 1 tablespoon soy sauce
 1 medium-size head bok choy
 2 to 3 teaspoons sesame seeds
 ¼ cup salad oil
 1 clove garlic, minced or pressed
 ¼ cup water

Prepare Cooking Sauce and set aside.

Cut beef with the grain into 1½-inch-wide strips; then cut each strip across the grain into ⅛-inch-thick slanting slices. Place meat in a bowl, stir in soy, and let marinate for 15 minutes.

Meanwhile, cut bok choy leaves from stems. Cut stems diagonally into ¼-inch slices; coarsely shred leaves. Set stems and leaves aside separately; you should have 6 to 8 cups *total* lightly packed stems and leaves.

Place a wok over medium heat. When wok is hot, add sesame seeds and stir until golden (about 2 minutes); remove from wok and set aside. Increase heat to high. Add 2 tablespoons of the oil to wok; when oil is hot, add garlic and bok choy stems. Stir-fry for 1 to 2 minutes. Add water, then cover and cook for 2 minutes; add bok choy leaves and cook, uncovered, stirring occasionally, just until leaves and stems are tender to bite (1 to 2 more minutes). Remove from wok and set aside.

Pour remaining 2 tablespoons oil into wok. When oil is hot, add meat; stir-fry until browned (1½ to 2 minutes). Return bok choy to wok. Stir sauce and add, then add sesame seeds. Cook, stirring, until sauce boils and thickens. Makes 2 or 3 servings.

Cooking Sauce. Stir together ¾ cup **regular-strength chicken broth**, 4 teaspoons **cornstarch**, 2 teaspoons **soy sauce**, 1 teaspoon minced **fresh ginger** or ½ teaspoon ground ginger, and 2 tablespoons **dry sherry**.

Per serving: 407 calories, 32 g protein, 14 g carbohydrates, 26 g total fat, 65 mg cholesterol, 1,081 mg sodium

Oyster Beef

Preparation time: About 15 minutes, plus 30 minutes to soak mushrooms

Marinating time: 15 minutes

Cooking time: About 7 minutes

This tasty beef dish gains subtle flavor from oyster sauce—a thick brown sauce sold in Asian markets and well-stocked supermarkets.

 6 medium-size dried Oriental mushrooms
 ¾ pound lean boneless beef steak (such as top round, flank, or sirloin)
 1 tablespoon *each* dry sherry and soy sauce
 2 tablespoons water
 ¼ teaspoon sugar
 2 teaspoons cornstarch
 3½ tablespoons salad oil
    Cooking Sauce (recipe follows)
 1 clove garlic, minced
 ½ teaspoon minced fresh ginger
 ½ cup sliced bamboo shoots
    Salt

Soak mushrooms in warm water to cover for 30 minutes, then drain. Cut off and discard stems; squeeze caps dry, thinly slice, and set aside.

Cut beef with the grain into 1½-inch-wide strips; then cut each strip across the grain into ⅛-inch-thick slanting slices. In a bowl, stir together sherry, soy, 1 tablespoon of the water, sugar, and cornstarch. Add beef and stir to coat, then stir in 1½ teaspoons of the oil and let marinate for 15 minutes.

Meanwhile, prepare Cooking Sauce and set aside.

Place a wok over high heat; when wok is hot, add 2 tablespoons of the oil. When oil begins to heat, add garlic and ginger and stir once. Add beef mixture and stir-fry until meat is browned (1½ to 2 minutes); remove from wok and set aside.

Pour remaining 1 tablespoon oil into wok. When oil is hot, add bamboo shoots and mushrooms; stir-fry for 1 minute. Add remaining 1 tablespoon water, cover, and cook for 2 minutes. Return meat mixture to wok. Stir Cooking Sauce, add to wok, and stir until sauce boils and thickens. Season to taste with salt. Makes 4 servings.

Cooking Sauce. Stir together 2 tablespoons **oyster sauce,** 1 tablespoon **cornstarch,** and ½ cup **regular-strength chicken broth.**

Per serving: 268 calories, 22 g protein, 9 g carbohydrates, 16 g total fat, 49 mg cholesterol, 787 mg sodium

Asparagus Beef

Follow directions for **Oyster Beef,** but substitute 1 pound **asparagus** for mushrooms and bamboo shoots. To prepare asparagus, snap off and discard tough ends of spears, then cut spears into ½-inch slanting slices.

Two-Onion Beef

Follow directions for **Oyster Beef,** but substitute 1 large **onion** and 12 **green onions** (including tops) for mushrooms and bamboo shoots. Cut onion in half, then thinly slice; cut green onions into 1½-inch lengths. After removing beef from wok, stir-fry sliced onion for 1 minute. Then add green onions and stir-fry for 30 seconds before returning beef to wok.

Beef & Broccoli

Preparation time: About 20 minutes

Marinating time: 15 minutes

Cooking time: About 15 minutes

Ginger and ground red pepper heat up the hearty sauce that coats beef strips and tender broccoli. Make the cooking sauce while the beef marinates.

- ¾ **pound broccoli**
- 1 **pound lean boneless beef steak (such as top round, flank, or sirloin)**
- 2 **tablespoons soy sauce**
- 1 **clove garlic, minced or pressed**
  Cooking Sauce (recipe follows)
- ¼ **cup salad oil**
- 2 **tablespoons water**

Cut off and discard tough ends of broccoli stalks; peel stalks, if desired. Cut tops into small flowerets; slice stalks ¼ inch thick. Set aside.

Cut beef with the grain into 1½-inch-wide strips, then cut each strip across the grain into ¼-inch-thick slanting slices. In a bowl, mix beef, soy, and garlic. Let marinate for 15 minutes. Meanwhile, prepare Cooking Sauce and set aside.

Place a wok over high heat; when wok is hot, add 1 tablespoon of the oil. When oil is hot, add half the meat mixture and stir-fry until meat is browned (2 to 3 minutes); remove from wok and set aside. Repeat to brown remaining meat, using 1 tablespoon more oil.

Pour remaining 2 tablespoons oil into wok. When oil is hot, add broccoli and stir-fry for about 1 minute. Add water, cover, and cook, stirring fre-

quently, until broccoli is tender-crisp to bite (about 3 more minutes). Stir Cooking Sauce, then add to wok along with meat; stir until sauce boils and thickens. Makes 3 or 4 servings.

Cooking Sauce. Stir together 1½ tablespoons **cornstarch,** ¼ teaspoon **ground ginger,** a dash of **ground red pepper** (cayenne), 2 tablespoons **dry sherry,** and 1¼ cups **regular-strength beef broth.**

Per serving: 318 calories, 29 g protein, 8 g carbohydrates, 19 g total fat, 65 mg cholesterol, 879 mg sodium

Steak Paprikash

Preparation time: About 10 minutes

Cooking time: About 15 minutes

A traditional slow-simmered dish from central Europe is easily adapted to stir-frying—with delicious results (and a considerable savings of time).

- 6 **slices bacon**
- 1½ **pounds lean boneless beef steak (such as top round, flank, or sirloin), cut across the grain into ¼-inch-thick slices**
- 1 **large onion, thinly sliced**
- 1 **small head green cabbage (about 1½ lbs.), coarsely shredded**
- 1 **tablespoon paprika**
- 2 **tablespoons water**
- 1 **cup** *each* **sour cream and plain yogurt**
- 2 **tablespoons all-purpose flour**
- 2 **tablespoons minced parsley**

Place a wok over medium heat; when wok is hot, add bacon. Cook, turning as needed, until crisp (about 3 minutes). Lift from wok, drain, crumble, and set aside. Pour off and discard all but 2 tablespoons of the drippings.

Place wok with bacon drippings over high heat. When fat is hot, add half the beef and stir-fry just until browned (2 to 3 minutes); with a slotted spoon, transfer meat to a bowl. Repeat to brown remaining beef.

Add onion, cabbage, and paprika to wok. Stir-fry for 1 minute; then add water, cover, and cook for 4 more minutes.

Stir together sour cream, yogurt, and flour; then stir into cabbage mixture. Add meat and any juices and stir just until hot. Top with bacon and parsley. Makes 4 servings.

Per serving: 565 calories, 50 g protein, 23 g carbohydrates, 31 g total fat, 138 mg cholesterol, 375 mg sodium

Note: Recipes may be prepared in either a skillet or a wok.

A visual feast of appetizing color, Tomato Beef
(recipe on facing page) shows off the wok's magic with
fresh ingredients. A touch of curry gives the spicy
sauce memorable flavor.

(Pictured on cover and facing page)

Tomato Beef

Preparation time: *About 20 minutes*

Marinating time: *15 minutes*

Cooking time: *About 7 minutes*

Tender strips of beef and crisply cooked vegetables are tossed with a curry-flavored sauce for this easy Cantonese dish.

- ¾ **pound lean boneless beef steak (such as top round, flank, or sirloin)**
- 2 teaspoons *each* **cornstarch and soy sauce**
- 1 tablespoon *each* **dry sherry and water**
- ¼ **cup salad oil**
  Cooking Sauce (recipe follows)
- ½ **teaspoon minced fresh ginger**
- 1 **clove garlic, minced**
- 2 **large stalks celery, cut into ¼-inch-thick slanting slices**
- 1 **medium-size onion, cut into wedges, layers separated**
- 1 **green bell pepper, seeded and cut into 1-inch squares**
- 3 **medium-size tomatoes,** *each* **cut into 6 wedges**
  Salt

Cut beef with the grain into 1½-inch-wide strips; then cut each strip across the grain into ⅛-inch-thick slanting slices. In a bowl, stir together cornstarch, soy, sherry, and water. Add meat and stir to coat, then stir in 1½ teaspoons of the oil and let marinate for 15 minutes.

Meanwhile, prepare Cooking Sauce and set aside.

Place a wok over high heat; when wok is hot, add 2 tablespoons of the oil. When oil begins to heat, add ginger and garlic and stir once. Add meat mixture and stir-fry until meat is browned (1½ to 2 minutes); remove from wok and set aside.

Pour remaining 1½ tablespoons oil into wok. When oil is hot, add celery and onion and stir-fry for 1 minute. Add bell pepper and stir-fry for 1 minute, adding a few drops of water if wok appears dry. Add tomatoes and stir-fry for 1 minute. Return meat to wok. Stir Cooking Sauce, pour into wok, and stir until sauce boils and thickens. Season to taste with salt. Makes 4 servings.

Cooking Sauce. Stir together 1 tablespoon *each* **soy sauce, Worcestershire,** and **cornstarch;** 3 tablespoons **catsup;** 1 teaspoon **curry powder;** and ½ cup **water.**

Per serving: 308 calories, 22 g protein, 16 g carbohydrates, 18 g total fat, 48 mg cholesterol, 679 mg sodium

Beef with Snow Peas

Preparation time: *About 25 minutes*

Marinating time: *2 hours*

Cooking time: *About 8 minutes*

This spicy stir-fry of beef and snow peas owes its complex flavors to a meat marinade of soy, sherry, sesame oil, hoisin sauce, and Tientsin preserved vegetables. You'll find the preserved vegetables—called *chong choy*— in Asian markets.

- 1 **pound lean boneless beef steak (such as top round, flank, or sirloin)**
  Spicy Marinade (recipe follows)
- ¼ **cup salad oil**
- ¾ **pound Chinese pea pods (also called snow or sugar peas) or sugar snap peas, ends and strings removed; or 2 packages (6 oz.** *each***) frozen Chinese pea pods, thawed and drained**
- 1 **tablespoon water**
- 1 **tablespoon soy sauce**
- 1 **teaspoon sugar**
- 1 **small onion, cut into slivers**

Cut beef into 1-inch chunks. With a mallet, pound each piece to a thickness of about ¼ inch. Prepare marinade; stir in beef, then cover and refrigerate for at least 2 hours or until next day.

Place a wok over high heat; when wok is hot, add 2 tablespoons of the oil. When oil is hot, add fresh pea pods. Stir-fry for about 3 minutes; add water, cover, and cook until pea pods are tender-crisp to bite—about 30 seconds. (If using frozen pea pods, simply stir-fry for 30 seconds *total*.) Transfer to a serving dish. Return wok to heat and add remaining 2 tablespoons oil; when oil is hot, add beef and marinade. Stir-fry until meat is browned (2 to 3 minutes). Stir in soy, sugar, and onion; cook for 1 more minute. Makes about 4 servings.

Spicy Marinade. Stir together 2 tablespoons **salad oil** and 1 tablespoon *each* **soy sauce, catsup, dry sherry, cornstarch, hoisin sauce,** and **sesame oil.** If desired, stir in 1 tablespoon **Tientsin preserved vegetables.** Then stir in 1 teaspoon **Worcestershire** and 1 clove **garlic,** minced or pressed.

Per serving: 436 calories, 29 g protein, 14 g carbohydrates, 29 g total fat, 65 mg cholesterol, 764 mg sodium

---

Note: Recipes may be prepared in either a skillet or a wok.

Glossary of Asian Ingredients

Because many wok recipes have Asian origins, some of the ingredients called for in this book may be unfamiliar to you. We describe a few of these ingredients here. All are sold in Asian markets, and several—dried mushrooms and five-spice—are stocked in most grocery stores.

Bean sauce. A thick brown sauce made from fermented soybeans, salt, flour, and sugar. Packaged in cans or jars, it's available in two forms: regular, which contains whole beans, and ground, which has a fairly smooth texture. Refrigerate in a tightly closed jar after opening.

Sweet bean sauce, sweeter than the standard product, can be replaced with hoisin sauce; *hot bean sauce* can be replaced with crushed dried hot red chiles or liquid hot pepper seasoning.

Bean threads. Thin, near-transparent strands made from ground mung beans, also sold as *harusame* and as cellophane, translucent, and shining noodles. Uncooked bean threads will keep indefinitely if stored in a cool, dry place. Before using in our recipes, soak in warm water until pliable (about 30 minutes).

Black beans. Small fermented black beans, preserved in salt and sold in small jars or plastic bags, are often used to flavor Chinese sauces. Store them in a tightly covered jar in a cool, dry place; rinse thoroughly before using.

Chili oil. Watch out: This orange red oil can be extremely hot. Sold in dispenser bottles, chili oil typically fires up stir-fry dishes; it's also served as a condiment.

Chinese five-spice. Widely available five-spice is a fragrant blend of ground cloves, fennel, licorice root, cinnamon, and star anise.

Chinese wheat flour noodles. Sometimes labeled *mein*; available fresh or dried. Use fresh noodles within a day or two, or freeze for longer storage; dried noodles will keep indefinitely in a cool, dry place. Any fresh or dried thin noodles or spaghetti can substitute for mein.

Coconut milk. Prepared coconut milk is available canned or frozen. If it's very thick, dilute it with water.

Dried mushrooms. Shiitake mushrooms are the most commonly sold type of dried Oriental mushrooms. Before using them, you'll need to soak them in warm water, then discard the woody stems.

Black fungus, also called cloud or tree ears, are small and crinkly —but when soaked, the "ears" expand dramatically. Before using the soaked fungus, pinch out the hard, knobby centers.

Stored in a cool, dry place, both dried mushrooms and black fungus will keep indefinitely.

Fish sauce. The Thai version (*nam pla*) of this thin, salty sauce is recommended for use in our recipes; it's much milder than the Vietnamese *nuoc mam*, which has an extremely strong odor and flavor. Store airtight in the refrigerator for up to several months.

Gyoza. Round pot sticker wrappers made from flour and water. Unopened, they'll keep in the refrigerator for up to 3 weeks; once opened, they should be used within a few days. Won ton skins can take the place of gyoza.

Hoisin sauce. Made from soybeans blended with flour, sugar, vinegar, and spices, brownish red hoisin sauce is used as both a cooking sauce and a condiment. It's available in cans or jars; the canned sauce should be transferred to an airtight jar after opening. Hoisin sauce will keep for several months in the refrigerator.

Oyster sauce. This thick brown sauce, available in most supermarkets, has a subtle oyster flavor. Refrigerate after opening (it will keep for several months).

Rice. *Long-grain rice* is preferred for Chinese and many Southeast Asian dishes; *short-grain rice*, slightly sticky when cooked, is favored by Japanese and Korean cooks.

Rice noodles. Also called rice sticks and *mai fun*, these slender strands are made from rice flour. Uncooked noodles will keep indefinitely if stored in a cool, dry place. Before using in our recipes, boil (see page 93).

Sesame oil. Golden brown and aromatic, this seasoning oil is pressed from toasted sesame seeds. Since it's strong, use it sparingly.

Tofu bean curd. This high-protein food is made from soybeans— soaked, cooked, and puréed, then coagulated into curd with epsom salts and vinegar. The custardy cakes come in soft, medium-firm, and firm consistencies. (Bean curd labeled "regular" has a medium-firm consistency.) Though quite bland on its own, bean curd readily absorbs the flavors of other foods, making it a useful extender. Rinse packaged curd after opening; then cover with cold water and refrigerate for up to a few days (change water daily).

Udon. Resembling square spaghetti, these thick wheat-flour noodles are usually sold dried. (Occasionally, though, you'll find fresh ones in Japanese markets; they freeze beautifully.) Dried udon will keep almost indefinitely if stored in a cool, dry place.

Simple Sauerbraten

Preparation time: 15 minutes

Marinating time: 30 minutes

Cooking time: About 10 minutes

Traditional sauerbraten is a tasty but time-consuming dish to prepare. Slicing the meat and stir-frying cuts down on the cooking time without sacrificing the familiar tangy flavor. Accompany this spicy sweet-and-sour main course with broccoli and buttered noodles.

- 1 **pound lean boneless beef steak (such as top round, flank, or sirloin)**
- ¼ **cup** *each* **dry white wine and white vinegar**
- 1 **tablespoon brown sugar**
- 1 **dry bay leaf**
- ¼ **teaspoon** *each* **pepper and ground cloves**
- 2 **tablespoons salad oil**
- 1 **red onion, thinly sliced**
- 1 **cup thinly sliced carrots**
- ½ **cup thinly sliced celery**
- 1 **clove garlic, minced or pressed**
- 2 **tablespoons water**
- ¼ **cup crushed gingersnaps**
  Sour cream, optional

Cut beef with the grain into 2-inch-wide strips; then cut each strip across the grain into ⅛-inch-thick slanting slices. In a bowl, mix wine, vinegar, brown sugar, bay leaf, pepper, and cloves; stir in meat and let marinate for about 30 minutes. Drain meat, reserving marinade, and remove bay leaf.

Place a wok over high heat; when wok is hot, add oil. When oil is hot, add meat and stir-fry until meat is browned (1½ to 2 minutes). Remove meat from wok; set aside. Immediately add red onion and carrots to wok and stir-fry for 1 minute. Add celery and garlic; stir-fry for 1 more minute. Add water, cover, and cook until carrots and celery are tender-crisp to bite (about 3 more minutes).

Return meat to wok and add marinade and gingersnaps. Stir until sauce thickens slightly. Serve with a dollop of sour cream, if desired. Makes 4 servings.

Per serving: 283 calories, 27 g protein, 15 g carbohydrates, 12 g total fat, 67 mg cholesterol, 123 mg sodium

Beef Provençal

Preparation time: 15 minutes

Marinating time: 30 minutes

Cooking time: About 5 minutes

The sunny flavors of southern France infuse this quick stir-fry. For top quality, look for golden-colored virgin olive oil made from the first pressing of ripe olives. Serve with boiled artichokes for a memorable meal from Provence.

- 1 **pound lean boneless beef steak (such as top round, flank, or sirloin)**
- 1 **onion, finely chopped**
- ½ **cup dry red wine**
- 1 **dry bay leaf**
- ½ **teaspoon dry thyme leaves**
- ¼ **teaspoon** *each* **pepper and ground cloves**
- 2 **tablespoons olive oil**
- 1 **clove garlic, minced or pressed**
- 1 **tablespoon flour**
- 1 **tomato, peeled, seeded, and chopped**
- 1 **tablespoon grated orange rind**
- 8 **oil-cured olives, pitted**
- 1 **tablespoon chopped parsley**

Cut beef with the grain into 2-inch-wide strips; then cut each strip across the grain into ⅛-inch-thick slanting slices. In a bowl, mix beef, onion, wine, bay leaf, thyme, pepper, and cloves. Let marinate for 30 minutes. Drain meat and onions, reserving marinade, and remove bay leaf.

Place a wok over high heat; when wok is hot, add oil. When oil is hot, add garlic and stir once. Add meat and onions. Stir-fry until meat is browned (1½ to 2 minutes).

Sprinkle meat with flour, stir once, and add marinade, tomato, orange rind, olives, and parsley. Stir until sauce thickens slightly. Makes 4 servings.

Per serving: 268 calories, 27 g protein, 7 g carbohydrates, 15 g total fat, 65 mg cholesterol, 327 mg sodium

(Pictured on facing page)
Fajitas Stir-fry

Preparation time: About 30 minutes

Cooking time: About 7 minutes

In this quick version of fajitas, the steak is stir-fried instead of grilled. You wrap the meat in warm flour tortillas—or crisp iceberg lettuce leaves.

    1 **pound lean boneless beef steak (such as
       top round, flank, or sirloin)**
    2 **tablespoons salad oil**
    2 **cloves garlic, minced or pressed**
    1 **large onion, thinly sliced and separated
       into rings**
    2 **or 3 fresh jalapeño chiles, seeded and
       minced**
    1 **large red bell pepper, seeded and cut into
       thin strips**
    2 **teaspoons ground cumin**
    3 **tablespoons lime juice**
    1 **teaspoon cornstarch**
    2 **medium-size Roma-type tomatoes, diced**
       Salt and pepper
       Lime wedges
       Sour cream (optional)
    1 **large ripe avocado, pitted, peeled, and
       diced**
    8 **warm flour tortillas (8-inch diameter); or
       8 large iceberg lettuce leaves, chilled**
       Homemade or purchased salsa (optional)

Cut beef with the grain into 1-inch-wide strips; then cut each strip across the grain into ⅛-inch-thick slices. Set aside.

Place a wok over high heat; when wok is hot, add 1 tablespoon of the oil. When oil is hot, add meat. Stir-fry until meat is browned (1½ to 2 minutes); transfer meat to a bowl with a slotted spoon.

Add remaining 1 tablespoon oil to wok, then add garlic, onion, chiles, and bell pepper. Stir-fry until onion is soft (about 3 minutes). Stir together cumin, lime juice, and cornstarch; add to wok. Return meat to wok, add tomatoes, and stir until mixture is hot and juices boil. Season to taste with salt and pepper, then pour fajitas into a serving dish; garnish with lime wedges. Offer sour cream (if desired) and avocado in separate dishes.

Spoon meat mixture onto tortillas or lettuce leaves; add sour cream, avocado, and a squeeze of lime to taste. Fold up and eat out of hand. Accompany with salsa, if desired. Makes 4 servings.

Per serving: 612 calories, 34 g protein, 49 g carbohydrates, 32 g total fat, 65 mg cholesterol, 76 mg sodium

Beef & Rice in Lettuce

Preparation time: About 10 minutes

Marinating time: 1½ hours

Cooking time: 8 minutes

Accompany tender soy-marinated steak strips with steamed rice—then wrap both meat and rice in lettuce for an eat-out-of-hand entrée. (You'll find instructions for steaming short-grain rice on page 68.)

    1   **tablespoon sesame seeds**
    2½ **tablespoons soy sauce**
    1   **tablespoon *each* sugar and sesame oil**
    2   **tablespoons thinly sliced green onion
        (including top)**
    1   **teaspoon *each* minced garlic and minced
        fresh ginger**
    1   **pound lean boneless beef steak (such as
        top round, flank, or sirloin)**
    2   **to 3 tablespoons salad oil**
        **About 2 cups steamed short-grain rice
        (such as pearl) or medium-grain rice**
    20 **to 32 red leaf lettuce leaves**
        Korean hot red pepper paste (optional)

Place a wok over medium heat. When wok is hot, add sesame seeds and stir until golden (about 2 minutes). Pour out of wok; crush thoroughly with a mortar and pestle or whirl briefly in a blender. Then pour into a bowl and stir in soy, sugar, sesame oil, onion, garlic, and ginger.

Cut beef across the grain into ⅛-inch-thick slices; add to soy mixture and stir to coat well. Cover and refrigerate for about 1½ hours. Drain, reserving marinade.

Place a wok over high heat; when wok is hot, add 2 tablespoons of the salad oil. When oil is hot, add about half the meat mixture and 1 to 2 tablespoons of the marinade. Stir-fry until meat is browned (1½ to 2 minutes). Remove from wok and keep warm. Repeat to brown remaining meat, adding more oil as needed and 1 to 2 tablespoons more marinade.

On each of 4 dinner plates, arrange about a fourth of the beef, about ½ cup of the rice, 5 to 8 lettuce leaves, and, if desired, a dab of red pepper paste. To eat, fill a lettuce leaf with meat, rice, and red pepper paste (if used). Roll up and eat out of hand. Makes 4 servings.

Per serving: 409 calories, 30 g protein, 30 g carbohydrates, 18 g total fat, 65 mg cholesterol, 706 mg sodium

Note: Recipes may be prepared in either a skillet or a wok.

Fajitas in a wok? Yes—when you make this hearty
stir-fried version of the Southwestern barbecue classic. Fun, delicious,
and quick, Fajitas Stir-fry (recipe on facing page)
is sure to become a favorite.

Sirloin Tips & Vegetables

Preparation time: About 10 minutes

Marinating time: About 30 minutes

Cooking time: About 8 minutes

Thin sirloin strips and vegetables, enhanced with ginger and hoisin, are served over spinach for an outstanding entrée. A red wine marinade both flavors and tenderizes the meat. You may use either fresh or frozen spinach; cook it just before you start to stir-fry.

    About 1 pound sirloin tips
¼ **cup dry red wine**
2 **tablespoons soy sauce**
1 **clove garlic, minced or pressed**
1 **teaspoon minced fresh ginger**
2 **tablespoons salad oil**
1 **cup thinly sliced celery**
½ **pound mushrooms, thinly sliced**
1 **can (about 8 oz.) water chestnuts, drained and sliced**
½ **cup thinly sliced green onions (including tops)**
2 **tablespoons hoisin sauce**
    Hot cooked spinach

Cut beef across the grain into ⅛-inch-thick strips and place in a shallow dish. Stir together wine, soy, garlic, and ginger; pour over meat and let marinate for about 30 minutes.

    Place a wok over high heat; when wok is hot, add oil. When oil is hot, add meat mixture and stir-fry until meat is browned (1½ to 2 minutes). Remove meat from wok and set aside. Immediately add celery, mushrooms, water chestnuts, onions, and hoisin. Stir-fry until celery is tender-crisp to bite (2 to 3 minutes). Return meat to wok; stir until heated through. Serve immediately over spinach. Makes 4 servings.

Per serving: 305 calories, 25 g protein, 14 g carbohydrates, 16 g total fat, 68 mg cholesterol, 352 mg sodium

Burgundy Beef

Preparation time: About 10 minutes

Marinating time: About 15 minutes

Cooking time: About 7 minutes

Nobody would describe *boeuf bourguignon* as a classic stir-fry—but this bold beef dish can in fact be made quite successfully in a wok. Wine and herbs flavor the distinctive sauce.

1 **pound lean boneless beef steak (such as top round, flank, or sirloin)**
¼ **pound mushrooms, thinly sliced**
½ **cup dry red wine**
2 **tablespoons salad oil**
¼ **teaspoon *each* dry chervil, dry tarragon, and salt**
⅛ **teaspoon dry marjoram leaves**
1½ **tablespoons all-purpose flour**

Cut beef with the grain into 2-inch-wide strips; then cut each strip across the grain into ⅛-inch-thick slanting slices. Combine meat and mushrooms in a bowl; stir in wine and let marinate at room temperature for about 15 minutes (or cover and refrigerate for up to 3 hours).

    Drain meat and mushrooms, reserving marinade. Place a wok over high heat; when wok is hot, add oil. When oil begins to heat, add chervil, tarragon, salt, and marjoram. Then add meat and mushrooms and stir-fry just until meat is browned (1½ to 2 minutes).

    Sprinkle meat mixture with flour, then blend in reserved marinade. Stir until sauce is slightly thickened. Makes 4 servings.

Per serving: 235 calories, 27 g protein, 4 g carbohydrates, 12 g total fat, 65 mg cholesterol, 197 mg sodium

Picadillo

Preparation time: About 5 minutes

Marinating time: 15 minutes

Cooking time: About 15 minutes

Picadillo is a South American specialty—"minced meat" (here, ground beef) served with a sweet and sour sauce and such traditional ingredients as olives, raisins, and bell peppers.

1 **pound lean ground beef**
1½ **tablespoons distilled white vinegar**
1 **clove garlic, minced or pressed**
1 **teaspoon ground cumin**
2 **tablespoons salad oil**
1 **small onion, chopped**
1 **small green bell pepper, seeded and cut into thin strips**
1 **can (8 oz.) tomato sauce**
½ **cup water**
½ **teaspoon cracked bay leaves**
6 **pimento-stuffed green olives, sliced**
1 **tablespoon raisins**
    Salt and pepper
1 **can (4 oz.) shoestring potatoes**

In a bowl, combine beef, vinegar, garlic, and cumin; mix well and let stand for 15 minutes.

Place a wok over medium-high heat; when wok is hot, add 1 tablespoon of the oil. When oil is hot, add meat mixture; cook, stirring, until meat is browned (about 3 minutes). Lift out and set aside; spoon out and discard any fat.

Pour remaining 1 tablespoon oil into wok; when oil is hot, add onion and bell pepper and stir-fry until onion is soft (about 4 minutes). Stir in tomato sauce, water, bay leaves, olives, and raisins. Bring to a boil; then reduce heat and simmer, uncovered, until slightly reduced (about 5 minutes). Add meat mixture and cook until heated through (about 2 more minutes). Season to taste with salt and pepper. Mound on a rimmed platter; surround with potatoes. Makes 4 servings.

Per serving: 378 calories, 22 g protein, 16 g carbohydrates, 26 g total fat, 69 mg cholesterol, 525 mg sodium

Lettuce Tacos

Preparation time: About 25 minutes

Cooking time: 8 to 10 minutes

Crisp lettuce leaves make a light, cool, change-of-pace wrapper for this spicy meat and vegetable mixture.

- 1 **medium-size head iceberg lettuce (about 1 lb.)**
- 1 **tablespoon salad oil**
- 2 **medium-size carrots, coarsely chopped**
- 1 **large zucchini (7 to 8 inches long), cut into ¼-inch cubes**
- 1 **cup fresh corn kernels cut from cob or 1 cup frozen whole-kernel corn, thawed and drained**
- 1 **pound lean ground beef**
- 2 **cloves garlic, minced or pressed**
- 1 **tablespoon chili powder**
- 1 **teaspoon ground cumin**
- 1 **cup thinly sliced green onions (including tops)**
- 1 **can (6 oz.) spicy tomato cocktail**
- 1 **tablespoon cornstarch**
  Salt
- ½ **cup shredded jack cheese**

Separate leaves from lettuce; rinse and shake dry. Arrange on a serving plate, cover, and refrigerate.

Place a wok over high heat; when wok is hot, add oil. When oil is hot, add carrots; stir-fry for 1 minute. Add zucchini and corn; stir-fry for 1 more minute, then remove vegetables with a slotted spoon and set aside.

Crumble beef into wok; cook, stirring, until browned (2 to 3 minutes). Spoon off and discard all but 1 tablespoon of the fat. Then add garlic, chili powder, cumin, and onions to meat; cook, stirring, just until onions begin to soften. Return carrot mixture to wok and stir until heated through.

Mix tomato cocktail and cornstarch; add to wok and cook, stirring, until sauce boils and thickens. Season to taste with salt. Transfer to a serving bowl; sprinkle with cheese.

To serve, spoon beef mixture onto chilled lettuce leaves. Makes 4 servings.

Per serving: 451 calories, 28 g protein, 24 g carbohydrates, 28 g total fat, 85 mg cholesterol, 342 mg sodium

Five-spice Pork & Potatoes

Preparation time: About 10 minutes

Cooking time: About 25 minutes

Russet potatoes and thin, tender pork strips soak up the fragrance and flavor of Chinese five-spice. The bottled spice blend is sold in many markets, but if you can't find it, you can easily make your own.

- 3 **large russet potatoes (about 1½ lbs. *total*)**
- 2 **tablespoons salad oil**
- 1 **pound lean boneless pork (such as shoulder or butt), trimmed of excess fat and cut into ¼- by 1- by 3-inch strips**
- 2 **cloves garlic, minced or pressed**
- 1½ **cups water**
- 3 **tablespoons soy sauce**
- 2 **teaspoons sugar**
- 1¼ **teaspoons Chinese five-spice; or ½ teaspoon ground ginger, ¼ teaspoon *each* ground cinnamon and crushed anise seeds, and ⅛ teaspoon *each* ground allspice and ground cloves**
- ⅓ **cup thinly sliced green onions (including tops)**

Peel potatoes and cut crosswise into ½-inch-thick slices; cut large slices in half. Set aside.

Place a wok over high heat; when wok is hot, add oil. When oil is hot, add pork and garlic. Stir-fry until pork is browned (2 to 3 minutes). Add potatoes, water, soy, sugar, and five-spice. Bring to a boil; then reduce heat, cover, and simmer, stirring occasionally, until potatoes are tender when pierced (about 20 minutes). Garnish with onions. Makes 3 or 4 servings.

Per serving: 359 calories, 26 g protein, 28 g carbohydrates, 16 g total fat, 76 mg cholesterol, 867 mg sodium

Note: Recipes may be prepared in either a skillet or a wok.

Instead of going out for Chinese food, you'll soon choose to
stay home and dine on spicy Twice-cooked Pork (recipe on
facing page). It really does involve double-cooking the pork,
but the flavor is well worth the extra time.

(Pictured on facing page)

Twice-cooked Pork

Preparation time: About 5 minutes

Cooking time: About 45 minutes to simmer; about 6 minutes to stir-fry

The pork in this spicy Szechwan dish really is cooked twice—first simmered, then stir-fried (if you like, you can even do the cooking on different days). Sweet and hot bean sauces add a distinctive flavor—but if you can't find them, you may use hoisin sauce and chiles with equally tasty results.

> 1 **pound lean boneless pork (such as shoulder or butt), in 1 piece**
> 1 **tablespoon dry sherry**
> 1 **thin, quarter-size slice fresh ginger, crushed with the side of a cleaver**
> 3 **green onions (including tops)**
> 2 **teaspoons hot bean sauce; or 2 small dried hot red chiles, crumbled**
> 4 **teaspoons sweet bean sauce or hoisin sauce**
> 1 **tablespoon soy sauce**
> 1 **teaspoon sugar**
> 2 **small green bell peppers or 1** *each* **small green and red bell pepper**
> 3 **tablespoons salad oil**
> ½ **teaspoon salt**
> 2 **cloves garlic, minced**
> 1 **teaspoon minced fresh ginger**

Place pork, sherry, and ginger slice in a 2-quart pan. Cut 1 of the green onions in half crosswise and add to pork, then add enough water to barely cover meat. Bring to a simmer; cover and simmer until meat is tender when pierced (about 45 minutes).

Lift meat from broth and refrigerate until cold. Then cut into 1½-inch-square pieces about ⅛ inch thick. (The fatty parts of the meat are considered a delicacy, but remove them if you wish.)

In a bowl, combine hot bean sauce, sweet bean sauce, soy, and sugar. Seed bell peppers and cut into 1-inch squares; cut remaining 2 green onions into 1-inch lengths.

Place a wok over high heat; when wok is hot, add 2 tablespoons of the oil. When oil is hot, add bell peppers and stir-fry for 1½ minutes, adding a few drops of water if wok appears dry. Sprinkle with salt and stir once, then remove peppers from wok. Add remaining 1 tablespoon oil to wok. When oil begins to heat, add garlic and minced ginger and stir once; then add pork and stir-fry for 1 minute. Add bean sauce mixture and toss until pork is coated with sauce. Return bell peppers to wok along with onion. Stir for 30 seconds to heat through. Makes 3 or 4 servings.

Per serving: 302 calories, 24 g protein, 8 g carbohydrates, 20 g total fat, 76 mg cholesterol, 790 mg sodium

Hawaiian Pork

Preparation time: About 15 minutes

Cooking time: About 20 minutes

Emerald-green snow peas and bright bell peppers add color and crisp texture to this richly flavored version of sweet and sour pork.

> **Sweet-Sour Sauce (recipe follows)**
> 2 **pounds lean boneless pork (such as shoulder or butt), trimmed of excess fat and cut into ¾-inch cubes**
> 1 **egg, beaten**
> **About ½ cup cornstarch**
> **About 6 tablespoons salad oil**
> 1 *each* **small green and red bell pepper, seeded and cut into 1-inch squares**
> 1 **small onion, cut into wedges, layers separated**
> ¼ **pound Chinese pea pods (also called snow or sugar peas) or sugar snap peas, ends and strings removed; or 1 package (6 oz.) frozen Chinese pea pods, thawed and drained**

Prepare Sweet-Sour Sauce; set aside.

Dip pork cubes in beaten egg, drain briefly, and roll in cornstarch to coat lightly; shake off excess.

Place a wok over high heat; when wok is hot, add 2 tablespoons of the oil. When oil is hot, add half the pork; stir-fry until evenly browned (5 to 7 minutes). Lift pork from wok and set aside. Repeat to brown remaining meat, adding more oil as needed.

Add remaining oil (about 2 tablespoons) to wok. Add bell peppers and onion; stir-fry until vegetables are tender-crisp to bite (about 2 minutes). Add pea pods; then stir sauce and add. Stir until sauce boils and thickens; return pork to wok and stir until heated through. Makes 6 to 8 servings.

Sweet-Sour Sauce. Stir together ½ cup *each* **cider vinegar,** firmly packed **brown sugar,** and **catsup;** ¼ cup *each* **cornstarch** and **unsweetened pineapple juice;** and 2 tablespoons **soy sauce.**

Per serving: 408 calories, 24 g protein, 33 g carbohydrates, 20 g total fat, 110 mg cholesterol, 535 mg sodium

---

Note: Recipes may be prepared in either a skillet or a wok.

Pork Tenderloin Normandy

Preparation time: About 15 minutes

Cooking time: About 10 minutes

Apple slices, onion, and sliced pork mingle in a creamy sauce sparked with Dijon mustard. A sprinkle of raisins adds a sweet finishing touch.

- ½ teaspoon *each* salt and dry oregano leaves
- ⅛ teaspoon pepper
- 3 tablespoons all-purpose flour
  About ¾ pound pork tenderloin, cut into ⅛-inch-thick, 1½-inch-wide slices
- ¼ cup butter or margarine
- 1 large onion, chopped
- 1 large Golden Delicious apple, cored and thinly sliced
- 2 tablespoons Dijon mustard
- 1 cup milk
- 2 tablespoons raisins
  Chopped parsley

Combine salt, oregano, pepper, and flour. Dredge pork in flour mixture; shake off excess. Set remaining flour mixture aside.

Place a wok over medium-high heat; when wok is hot, add 2 tablespoons of the butter. When butter is melted, add pork and stir-fry until browned (2 to 3 minutes); remove pork from wok and set aside.

Add remaining 2 tablespoons butter to wok; when butter is melted, add onion and stir-fry until soft (about 3 minutes). Add apple, then sprinkle in remaining flour mixture; stir-fry for about 1 minute. Stir in mustard and milk; bring to a boil, then return meat to wok and stir-fry for about 2 minutes. Stir in raisins and sprinkle with parsley. Makes 3 or 4 servings.

Per serving: 318 calories, 21 g protein, 22 g carbohydrates, 16 g total fat, 95 mg cholesterol, 686 mg sodium

Pork with Baby Corn

Preparation time: About 20 minutes

Marinating time: 15 minutes

Cooking time: About 8 minutes

Baby sweet corn is a treat in this quick Cantonese entrée. Sold canned or bottled, the tiny, tender ears of corn are available in Asian markets and in the imported food section of most supermarkets.

- 1 teaspoon *each* cornstarch and soy sauce
- 1 tablespoon dry sherry
- ¼ teaspoon pepper
- 1 pound lean boneless pork (such as shoulder or butt), trimmed of excess fat and cut into ⅛- by 1- by 2-inch strips
- ¼ cup salad oil
  Cooking Sauce (recipe follows)
- 2 cloves garlic, minced
- 1 small onion, cut into wedges, layers separated
- ¼ pound mushrooms, thinly sliced
- 1 can (about 1 lb.) whole baby sweet corn, drained
- 8 green onions (including tops), cut into 2-inch lengths

In a bowl, stir together cornstarch, soy, sherry, and pepper. Add pork and stir to coat. Stir in 1 teaspoon of the oil. Let marinate for 15 minutes. Meanwhile, prepare Cooking Sauce and set aside.

Place a wok over high heat; when wok is hot, add 2 tablespoons of the oil. When oil begins to heat, add garlic and stir once. Then add half the pork mixture and stir-fry until meat is lightly browned (1½ to 2 minutes); remove from wok. Repeat to brown remaining meat, using 1 tablespoon more oil.

Pour remaining 2 teaspoons oil into wok. When oil is hot, add onion pieces and mushrooms and stir-fry for 1 minute, adding a few drops of water if wok appears dry. Return meat mixture to wok, then add corn and green onions; stir-fry for 30 seconds. Stir Cooking Sauce, add to wok, and stir until sauce boils and thickens. Makes 4 servings.

Cooking Sauce. Stir together 1½ tablespoons **cornstarch,** 1 teaspoon *each* **sugar** and **vinegar,** ¼ teaspoon **salt,** 1 tablespoon **soy sauce,** and ¾ cup **regular-strength chicken broth** or water.

Per serving: 435 calories, 27 g protein, 32 g carbohydrates, 24 g total fat, 76 mg cholesterol, 1,064 mg sodium

Yu-shiang Pork

Preparation time: About 15 minutes

Marinating time: 15 minutes

Cooking time: About 8 minutes

Yu-shiang pork doesn't taste like fish—but because the seasonings used are typical of Szechwan fish cookery, the dish is often called fish-flavored pork.

1 teaspoon cornstarch
¼ teaspoon salt
   Dash of white pepper
1 tablespoon dry sherry
¾ pound lean boneless pork (such as shoulder or butt), trimmed of excess fat and cut into matchstick pieces
3½ tablespoons salad oil
   Cooking Sauce (recipe follows)
2 cloves garlic, minced
1 teaspoon minced fresh ginger
3 or 4 small dried hot red chiles
⅔ cup sliced bamboo shoots, cut into matchstick pieces
10 green onions (including tops), cut into 2-inch lengths

In a bowl, combine cornstarch, salt, white pepper, and sherry. Add pork and stir to coat; then stir in 1½ teaspoons of the oil. Let marinate for 15 minutes. Meanwhile, prepare Cooking Sauce; set aside.

Place a wok over high heat. When wok is hot, add 2 tablespoons of the oil. When oil begins to heat, add garlic, ginger, and chiles; stir once. Add pork mixture and stir-fry until meat is lightly browned (2 to 3 minutes); remove from wok.

Pour remaining 1 tablespoon oil into wok. When oil is hot, add bamboo shoots and onions and stir-fry for 1 minute. Return pork mixture to wok. Stir Cooking Sauce, pour into wok, and stir until sauce boils and thickens. Makes 4 servings.

Cooking Sauce. Stir together 1 tablespoon *each* **sugar, vinegar,** and **dry sherry;** 2 tablespoons **soy sauce;** 3 tablespoons **regular-strength chicken broth** or water; and 2 teaspoons **cornstarch.**

Per serving: 299 calories, 19 g protein, 13 g carbohydrates, 17 g total fat, 57 mg cholesterol, 766 mg sodium

Sweet & Sour Pork

Preparation time: About 15 minutes

Cooking time: About 25 minutes

Here's one Chinese dish that's familiar to just about everybody. Crisp, juicy chunks of pork and a colorful medley of vegetables and fruit combine in a tangy, ginger-spiked sauce.

   Sweet & Sour Sauce (recipe follows)
2 pounds lean boneless pork (such as shoulder or butt), trimmed of excess fat and cut into 1-inch cubes
1 egg, beaten
   About ½ cup cornstarch

   About 5 tablespoons salad oil
1 medium-size onion, cut into 1-inch cubes
2 medium-size carrots, cut into ¼-inch-thick slanting slices
1 clove garlic, minced or pressed
2 tablespoons water
1 green bell pepper, seeded and cut into 1-inch squares
½ cup fresh or drained canned pineapple chunks
2 medium-size tomatoes, cut into 1-inch cubes

Prepare Sweet & Sour Sauce; set aside.

Dip pork cubes in beaten egg, drain briefly, and roll in cornstarch to coat lightly; shake off excess.

Place a wok over medium-high heat. When wok is hot, add 3 tablespoons of the oil. When oil is hot, add half the pork and stir-fry until evenly browned (about 7 minutes); lift pork from wok and set aside. Repeat to brown remaining meat, adding more oil as needed.

Scrape away and discard any browned particles from sides and bottom of wok, but leave oil in wok. If necessary, add more oil to wok to make about 2 tablespoons total. Place wok over high heat. When oil is hot, add onion, carrots, and garlic; stir-fry for about 1 minute. Add water and bell pepper; cover and cook, stirring frequently, for about 2 minutes. Add pineapple, tomatoes, and pork; stir Sweet & Sour Sauce, then add. Stir until mixture boils and thickens (about 1 minute). Makes 6 servings.

Sweet & Sour Sauce. Stir together 1 tablespoon **cornstarch** and ⅓ cup firmly packed **brown sugar.** Then stir in ½ teaspoon minced **fresh ginger** or ¼ teaspoon ground ginger, 1 tablespoon *each* **soy sauce** and **dry sherry,** and ¼ cup *each* **wine vinegar** and **regular-strength chicken or beef broth.**

Per serving: 474 calories, 32 g protein, 31 g carbohydrates, 25 g total fat, 147 mg cholesterol, 358 mg sodium

Note: Recipes may be prepared in either a skillet or a wok.

Sausage Etouffée

Preparation time: About 25 minutes

Cooking time: About 35 minutes

Extra-rich, spicy, and filling! This Cajun entrée starts with a "black roux": a blend of flour and oil cooked until deep brown, then blended with minced vegetables.

 1 cup Black Roux (recipe follows)
 ½ pound bacon, chopped
 1 medium-size eggplant (¾ to 1 lb.), cut into ½-inch cubes
 ½ cup *each* chopped onion, chopped green bell pepper, and chopped celery
 1 clove garlic, minced or pressed
 1 pound kielbasa (Polish sausage), cut into ½-inch-thick slices
 ½ teaspoon black pepper
 ⅛ teaspoon ground red pepper (cayenne)
 1½ cups water
 Salt
 ½ cup sliced green onions (including tops)

Prepare roux; set aside.

 Place a wok over medium heat; when wok is hot, add bacon and cook until crisp (about 3 minutes). Lift out with a slotted spoon and set aside; spoon out and discard all but 3 tablespoons of the drippings. Add eggplant to wok; stir often until eggplant is soft when pressed (about 5 minutes). Add bacon, chopped onion, bell pepper, celery, and garlic; stir-fry until onion is soft (about 4 minutes). Add sausage and stir-fry until hot. Mix in roux, black pepper, red pepper, and water; bring to a boil over high heat. Season to taste with salt, sprinkle with green onions, and serve. Makes 4 to 6 servings.

Black Roux. In a bowl, mix 1 cup **salad oil** and 1 cup **all-purpose flour** until smoothly blended. Place a wok over medium-high heat; when wok is hot, add oil-flour mixture. Using a spoon with a long wooden or heat-resistant handle, stir until mixture is dark brown to red-brown in color and smells darkly toasted (about 15 minutes); if it begins to smell burned, immediately remove wok from heat, let cool, discard roux, and start again.

 All at once add ¾ cup *each* finely chopped **onion** and finely chopped **green bell pepper** and ⅓ cup finely chopped **celery** to hot roux. Then remove wok from heat and stir until roux is no longer bubbly (2 to 3 minutes).

Per serving: 791 calories, 18 g protein, 26 g carbohydrates, 69 g total fat, 67 mg cholesterol, 884 mg sodium

---

(Pictured on facing page)

Papaya & Sausage Sauté

Preparation time: About 10 minutes

Cooking time: About 12 minutes

If you like meat and fruit together, be sure to try this unusual dish: succulent papaya slices and sausage rounds tumbled in a spicy honey glaze. When papayas aren't in season (or if you can't find them at the market), try making the sauté with apples instead.

 1¼ pounds mild Italian sausages, cut into ½-inch-thick slices
 2 tablespoons *each* lemon juice and honey
 ½ teaspoon *each* ground ginger, ground coriander, and curry powder
 2 medium-size papayas (about 1 lb. *each*), peeled, seeded, and cut lengthwise into ½-inch-thick slices
 Green onions (roots and any wilted tops trimmed) and minced green onion tops (optional)

Place a wok over high heat; when wok is hot, add sausage. Stir-fry until browned (about 3 minutes). Discard all but 3 tablespoons of the drippings. Push sausage to side of wok; stir lemon juice, honey, ginger, coriander, and curry powder into drippings at bottom of wok. Then push sausage into spice mixture and toss to coat; transfer to a serving plate and keep warm.

 Add papayas to wok. Cook over high heat, turning occasionally, until fruit is glazed and light brown (3 to 5 minutes). Arrange papayas around sausage. Garnish with whole and minced green onions, if desired. Makes about 4 servings.

Per serving: 499 calories, 22 g protein, 26 g carbohydrates, 35 g total fat, 88 mg cholesterol, 1,012 mg sodium

Apple & Sausage Sauté

Follow directions for **Papaya & Sausage Sauté,** but substitute 2 large **green-skinned apples,** cored and cut into ½-inch-thick slices, for papayas. Add ½ cup **toasted whole blanched almonds** along with apples.

Note: Recipes may be prepared in either a skillet or a wok.

Rich flavors mingle in Papaya & Sausage Sauté
(recipe on facing page). Brought together in a spicy honey glaze,
hearty bites of Italian sausage and smooth papaya slices
make an exquisite entrée.

Italian Veal with Peppers

Preparation time: About 15 minutes

Cooking time: About 15 minutes

Red and green bell peppers give this zesty entrée its great eye appeal. Quick preparation is another plus—making the dish takes only about half an hour from start to finish.

1 **pound boneless veal, cut into ¼-inch-thick slices**
  All-purpose flour
  About 3 tablespoons butter or margarine
  About 3 tablespoons salad oil
2 **large red or green bell peppers (or 1 *each* large red and green bell pepper), seeded and cut into ½-inch-wide strips**
1 **teaspoon dry oregano leaves**
1 **clove garlic, minced or pressed**
⅔ **cup dry white wine**
  Salt and pepper

Trim and discard any fat and membrane from veal; then cut meat into pieces about 1½ inches square. Dredge veal squares in flour to coat lightly; shake off excess. Set aside.

Place a wok over medium heat; when wok is hot, add 1 tablespoon *each* of the butter and oil. When butter is melted, add bell pepper strips, oregano, and garlic; stir-fry until peppers are soft when pierced (about 5 minutes). With a slotted spoon, transfer pepper mixture to a serving dish; keep warm.

Increase heat to medium-high; add 1 tablespoon *each* more butter and oil. When butter is melted, add about half the veal squares and stir-fry just until lightly browned on both sides (about 2 minutes). Arrange cooked veal in dish with bell peppers. Repeat to brown remaining veal squares, adding remaining butter and oil as needed to prevent sticking.

Pour wine into wok; bring to a boil. Boil, stirring to scrape browned bits free, until liquid is reduced by about half. Season sauce to taste with salt and pepper; pour over veal and peppers. Makes 4 servings.

Per serving: 383 calories, 23 g protein, 6 g carbohydrates, 29 g total fat, 104 mg cholesterol, 169 mg sodium

Veal & Asparagus Platter

Preparation time: About 15 minutes

Cooking time: About 25 minutes

Veal and fresh asparagus are topped with creamy mushroom sauce in an elegant entrée for entertaining. For a showy touch, you can flame the sauce with brandy.

1½ **pounds boneless veal, cut into ¼-inch-thick slices**
  Salt and pepper
  All-purpose flour
  About ¼ cup butter or margarine
  About 2 tablespoons salad oil
2 **pounds asparagus**
½ **pound mushrooms, cut into ¼-inch-thick slices**
2 **tablespoons brandy (optional)**
½ **teaspoon *each* dry tarragon and dry mustard**
⅔ **cup half-and-half or light cream**
1 **tablespoon lemon juice**

Trim and discard any fat and membrane from veal. Place veal between 2 sheets of wax paper on a cutting board or work surface. Pound with a flat-surfaced meat mallet until meat is about ⅛ inch thick. Cut into ¾-inch-wide strips; sprinkle lightly with salt and pepper, then dust with flour and shake off excess.

Place a wok over medium heat; when wok is hot, add 1 tablespoon *each* of the butter and oil. When butter is melted, add about half the veal and stir-fry until lightly browned (about 2 minutes). Transfer to a warm platter; keep warm. Repeat to brown remaining veal, adding about 1 tablespoon *each* more butter and oil as needed to prevent sticking.

Snap off and discard tough ends of asparagus. Rinse spears, then immerse in 1½ inches boiling water and cook, uncovered, just until tender to bite (5 to 7 minutes). Drain well; arrange on platter with veal.

Place wok over medium heat; when wok is hot, add remaining 2 tablespoons butter. When butter is melted, add mushrooms and stir-fry until lightly browned (about 3 minutes). Stir in 1 tablespoon flour; stir for 1 minute.

If using brandy, pour into a small pan. Warm over low heat until bubbly; carefully ignite (not beneath an exhaust fan or near flammable items) and pour into wok. When flames die down, add tarragon, mustard, and half-and-half. Stir until sauce is bubbly and thickened. Remove from heat, stir in lemon juice, and pour over veal and asparagus. Makes 6 servings.

Per serving: 367 calories, 27 g protein, 8 g carbohydrates, 26 g total fat, 111 mg cholesterol, 170 mg sodium

Green Beans with Lamb Sauce

Preparation time: About 15 minutes

Cooking time: About 30 minutes

Crisp green beans topped with a tomato-lamb sauce and dusted with Parmesan make an especially colorful entrée. Another time, try serving the sauce over steamed asparagus.

> 1 can (2 oz.) anchovy fillets
> 2 tablespoons salad oil
> 1 medium-size onion, minced
> 1 pound lean ground lamb
> 1 can (about 14 oz.) pear-shaped tomatoes
> ¼ pound cooked ham, minced
> 1 tablespoon drained capers
> ¼ teaspoon crushed dried hot red chiles
> 2 pounds green beans, ends removed
> ⅓ cup grated Parmesan cheese

Drain anchovy fillets. Set 3 fillets aside; mince remaining anchovies and set aside separately.

Place a wok over high heat; when wok is hot, add oil. When oil is hot, add onion and stir-fry until soft (about 3 minutes).

Crumble in lamb; stir-fry until browned (about 5 minutes). Spoon off and discard fat. With scissors, snip tomatoes in can into chunks. Add tomatoes and their liquid, minced anchovies, ham, capers, and chiles to meat mixture. Reduce heat and simmer, uncovered, stirring often, until sauce is almost dry (about 20 minutes).

Meanwhile, immerse beans in 1½ inches boiling water; cover and boil until tender-crisp to bite (5 to 10 minutes). Drain, arrange on a warm platter, and keep warm.

Spoon lamb sauce over beans; sprinkle with cheese and top with whole anchovy fillets. Makes 4 servings.

Per serving: 416 calories, 37 g protein, 20 g carbohydrates, 22 g total fat, 107 mg cholesterol, 939 mg sodium

Quick Lamb Curry

Preparation time: About 10 minutes

Cooking time: About 20 minutes

This is a mild curry, but if you enjoy fiery flavors, you can boost the heat with cayenne pepper. Complement the dish with your choice of condiments— raisins, coconut, peanuts, and more.

> 1 tablespoon salad oil
> 1 pound lean ground lamb
> 2 cloves garlic, minced or pressed
> 1 large onion, chopped
> 1 medium-size carrot, thinly sliced
> 1 small green bell pepper, seeded and cut into ½-inch-wide strips
> 1 tablespoon curry powder
> ½ teaspoon *each* ground ginger and ground cumin
> 1 small apple, peeled, cored, and thinly sliced
> 1 can (14½ oz.) regular-strength beef broth
>   Salt and ground red pepper (cayenne)
>   Condiments (suggestions follow)

Place a wok over medium heat; when wok is hot, add oil. When oil is hot, crumble in lamb and cook, stirring, until meat is browned (about 5 minutes). Spoon off and discard all but 2 tablespoons of the fat. Add garlic, onion, carrot, bell pepper, curry powder, ginger, and cumin; stir-fry until onion is soft (about 4 minutes). Add apple and stir-fry for 1 minute.

Stir in broth and simmer, uncovered, until vegetables are tender when pierced and sauce is slightly thickened (about 10 minutes). Season to taste with salt and red pepper. Serve with condiments of your choice. Makes 4 servings.

Condiments. Choose 3 or 4 of the following: sliced **bananas, chutney, plain yogurt,** chopped **peanuts,** shredded **coconut, raisins.**

Per serving: 226 calories, 23 g protein, 11 g carbohydrates, 8 g total fat, 79 mg cholesterol, 504 mg sodium

Note: Recipes may be prepared in either a skillet or a wok.

In Chicken with Black Bean Sauce (recipe on facing page),
tender morsels of breast meat contrast with brilliant bell pepper chunks.
Garlic, fermented black beans, and a soy-based sauce contribute to this
Cantonese feast of color and flavor.

Chicken & Turkey

(Pictured on facing page)

Chicken with Black Bean Sauce

Preparation time: About 15 minutes

Marinating time: 15 minutes

Cooking time: About 10 minutes

Depending on your preference, you can make this Cantonese dish with asparagus or bell peppers. Serve with hot rice and garnish with cilantro sprigs, if you like.

- 1 teaspoon *each* cornstarch and soy sauce
- 4 teaspoons water
- 2 teaspoons dry sherry
- 1 whole chicken breast (about 1 lb.), skinned, boned, and cut into bite-size pieces
- 3½ tablespoons salad oil
  Cooking Sauce (recipe follows)
- 1 pound red or green bell peppers or 1 pound asparagus
- 2 teaspoons fermented salted black beans, rinsed, drained, and finely chopped
- 1 large clove garlic, minced
- 1 medium-size onion, cut into wedges, layers separated

In a bowl, stir together cornstarch, soy, 1 teaspoon of the water, and sherry. Add chicken and stir to coat; then stir in 1½ teaspoons of the oil and let marinate for 15 minutes.

Meanwhile, prepare Cooking Sauce; set aside. Seed bell peppers and cut into 1-inch squares. (Or snap off and discard tough ends of asparagus; cut spears into ½-inch slanting slices.)

Place a wok over high heat; when wok is hot, add 2 tablespoons of the oil. When oil begins to heat, add black beans and garlic; stir once. Add chicken mixture and stir-fry until meat is no longer pink in center; cut to test (about 3 minutes). Remove from wok and set aside.

Pour remaining 1 tablespoon oil into wok; when oil is hot, add bell peppers and onion and stir-fry for 1 minute. Add remaining 1 tablespoon water and cook, uncovered, until vegetables are tender-crisp to bite—2 to 4 more minutes. (If using asparagus, add 2 tablespoons water; cook, covered, for 3 to 4 minutes.) Return chicken to wok. Stir Cooking Sauce, pour into wok, and stir until sauce boils and thickens. Makes 2 or 3 servings.

Cooking Sauce. Stir together 1 tablespoon *each* **soy sauce** and **cornstarch,** ¼ teaspoon **sugar,** and ½ cup **regular-strength chicken broth** or water.

Per serving: 320 calories, 25 g protein, 14 g carbohydrates, 18 g total fat, 57 mg cholesterol, 791 mg sodium

Jeweled Chicken

Preparation time: About 15 minutes

Cooking time: About 7 minutes

Fragrant lychees, spicy crystallized ginger, and slices of preserved kumquat bejewel this sweet-sour stir-fry. Look for the fruits in the gourmet or specialty foods section of your supermarket.

- 1 egg white
  Cornstarch
- 2 whole chicken breasts (about 1 lb. *each*), skinned, boned, and cut into ½- by 2-inch strips
- ¼ cup soy sauce
- 1 can (about 20 oz.) lychees
- 2 tablespoons *each* vinegar and sugar
- ¼ cup salad oil
- 1½ tablespoons minced crystallized ginger
  Fresh cilantro (coriander) sprigs
  Sliced kumquats preserved in syrup

In a bowl, beat together egg white and 2 tablespoons cornstarch. Add chicken and stir to coat. Set aside.

In another bowl, gradually blend soy with 1 tablespoon cornstarch. Drain lychees, reserving 6 tablespoons of the syrup; add reserved syrup to soy mixture along with vinegar and sugar.

Place a wok over high heat; when wok is hot, add 2 tablespoons of the oil. When oil is hot, add half the chicken mixture and stir-fry until meat is no longer pink in center; cut to test (about 3 minutes). Remove from wok and set aside. Repeat to cook remaining chicken, adding remaining 2 tablespoons oil.

Return all chicken to wok; blend in ginger, drained lychees, and soy mixture. Stir until sauce boils and thickens. Garnish with cilantro and kumquats. Makes 4 servings.

Per serving: 456 calories, 37 g protein, 43 g carbohydrates, 16 g total fat, 86 mg cholesterol, 1,190 mg sodium

Note: Recipes may be prepared in either a skillet or a wok.

Sweet & Sour Chicken in Pineapple Shells

Preparation time: About 30 minutes

Cooking time: About 10 minutes

Pineapple shells make attractive individual serving dishes for hot rice and a stir-fry of chicken, pepper strips, and juicy pineapple chunks.

- 2 **small pineapples (about 3 lbs.** *each***)**
  Sweet & Sour Sauce (recipe follows)
- 3 **tablespoons salad oil**
- 1 **clove garlic, minced or pressed**
- 1¾ **pounds chicken breasts, skinned, boned, and cut into ½- by 2-inch strips**
- 1 **medium-size onion, thinly sliced**
- 1 **medium-size green bell pepper, seeded and cut into thin strips**
  About 4 cups hot cooked rice
  Fresh cilantro (coriander) sprigs (optional)

Cut each pineapple in half lengthwise, cutting through crown. With a curved, serrated knife such as a grapefruit knife, cut fruit from peel, leaving shells intact; turn shells upside down to drain. Trim away core from fruit, then cut fruit into chunks about ½ inch thick. You'll need 3 cups pineapple chunks; reserve any remaining fruit for another use.

Just before cooking, drain the 3 cups pineapple chunks; reserve juice for another use. Also prepare Sweet & Sour Sauce and set aside.

Place a wok over high heat; when wok is hot, add 1 tablespoon of the oil. When oil is hot, add garlic and half the chicken and stir-fry until chicken is no longer pink in center; cut to test (about 3 minutes). Remove from wok and set aside. Repeat to cook remaining chicken, adding 1 tablespoon more oil.

Pour remaining 1 tablespoon oil into wok. When oil is hot, add onion and bell pepper. Stir-fry until vegetables are tender-crisp to bite (about 2 minutes).

Return chicken to wok. Stir Sweet & Sour Sauce; pour into wok along with pineapple. Stir until sauce boils and thickens.

Spoon equal portions of the chicken mixture into each of the 4 pineapple shells, mounding mixture at 1 end of shells. Spoon about 1 cup of the rice alongside chicken in each shell. Garnish with cilantro, if desired. Pour any extra chicken mixture into a serving bowl; offer at the table. Makes 4 servings.

Sweet & Sour Sauce. Stir together 4 teaspoons **cornstarch;** ¼ cup *each* **sugar, wine vinegar,** and **regular-strength chicken broth;** 2 tablespoons minced **fresh cilantro** (coriander) or 1½ teaspoons dry cilantro leaves; 2 tablespoons **catsup;** 1 tablespoon *each* **soy sauce** and **dry sherry;** ½ teaspoon **ground ginger;** and ¼ teaspoon *each* **salt** and **crushed red pepper.**

Per serving: 603 calories, 36 g protein, 85 g carbohydrates, 13 g total fat, 75 mg cholesterol, 634 mg sodium

Hot & Sour Chicken

Preparation time: About 15 minutes

Cooking time: About 10 minutes

Peppery-hot foods are favored in the Chinese province of Hunan—a preference reflected in this spicy dish. Season the sauce with purchased red pepper flakes, if you like, or use crushed whole dried chiles (remove the seeds for a milder flavor).

- **Cooking Sauce (recipe follows)**
- 2 **teaspoons** *each* **cornstarch, dry sherry, and salad oil**
- ¼ **teaspoon pepper**
- 1½ **to 1¾ pounds chicken breasts, skinned, boned, and cut into ¾-inch cubes**
- 2 **to 3 tablespoons salad oil**
- 1 **tablespoon finely chopped garlic**
- 2 **teaspoons finely chopped fresh ginger**
- 1 **tablespoon fermented salted black beans, rinsed, drained, and patted dry**
- 1 **green bell pepper, seeded and cut into 1-inch squares**
- 1 **carrot, thinly sliced**
- 1 **can (about 8 oz.) sliced bamboo shoots, drained**

Prepare Cooking Sauce and set aside. In a bowl, stir together cornstarch, sherry, the 2 teaspoons oil, and pepper. Add chicken and stir to coat.

Place a wok over high heat; when wok is hot, add 2 tablespoons of the oil. When oil is hot, add chicken mixture; stir-fry for 2 minutes. Add 1 tablespoon more oil, if needed; then add garlic, ginger, and black beans. Stir-fry until chicken is lightly browned (about 2 more minutes). Then add bell pepper, carrot, and bamboo shoots; stir-fry for 2 minutes. Stir sauce and add; stir until sauce boils and thickens. Makes 4 servings.

Cooking Sauce. Stir together 2 teaspoons **cornstarch,** ½ teaspoon **crushed dried hot red chiles,** 2 tablespoons **soy sauce,** 2½ tablespoons **white wine vinegar,** and ½ cup **regular-strength chicken broth.**

Per serving: 302 calories, 32 g protein, 9 g carbohydrates, 15 g total fat, 75 mg cholesterol, 843 mg sodium

Chicken Breasts with Papaya & Chutney

Preparation time: About 15 minutes

Cooking time: About 10 minutes

A tangy, chutney-based glaze coats tender chicken and sweet papaya. Present this richly flavored entrée on a bed of hot cooked spinach.

- 3 tablespoons salad oil
- ½ cup sliced almonds
- 3 whole chicken breasts (about 1 lb. *each*), skinned, boned, and split
- 1 large papaya
- 1½ tablespoons lime or lemon juice
- ½ cup Major Grey's chutney, finely chopped
- ½ cup regular-strength chicken broth
- 1 teaspoon cornstarch
- ½ teaspoon *each* paprika and ground ginger
- 2 tablespoons butter or margarine
  White pepper
  Hot cooked spinach

Place a wok over medium heat; when wok is hot, add 1 tablespoon of the oil. When oil is hot, add almonds and stir until golden (about 2 minutes). Remove from wok and set aside.

Rinse chicken and pat dry. Cut each breast half across the grain into ½-inch-wide strips; set aside.

Peel and halve papaya; remove seeds. Cut each papaya half lengthwise into quarters, then cut each piece in half crosswise. Place in a bowl, add lime juice, and stir until fruit is coated. In another bowl, stir together chutney, broth, cornstarch, paprika, and ginger.

Place wok over medium-high heat. When wok is hot, add 1 tablespoon *each* of the butter and oil. When butter is melted, add half the chicken and stir-fry until meat is no longer pink in center; cut to test (about 3 minutes). Remove from wok and set aside. Repeat to cook remaining chicken, adding remaining 1 tablespoon *each* butter and oil. Return all chicken to wok.

Stir chutney mixture and add to chicken. Bring to a boil and stir until thickened (about 2 minutes). Add papaya and stir gently just until fruit is glazed and heated through. Season to taste with white pepper.

To serve, spoon chicken mixture over spinach; sprinkle with almonds. Makes 6 servings.

Per serving: 388 calories, 36 g protein, 23 g carbohydrates, 17 g total fat, 96 mg cholesterol, 267 mg sodium

Watercress Chicken with Mushrooms

Preparation time: About 15 minutes

Cooking time: About 15 minutes

Vivid fresh watercress, mushrooms, and chunks of chicken breast combine in this simple stir-fry. For extra taste and texture, add a few teaspoons of toasted sesame seeds.

- ½ pound watercress
  Cooking Sauce (recipe follows)
- 2 whole chicken breasts (about 1 lb. *each*), skinned, boned, and cut into 1-inch chunks
- 2 cloves garlic, minced or pressed
- ¼ teaspoon *each* pepper and ground ginger
- 2 to 3 teaspoons sesame seeds (optional)
- 5 tablespoons salad oil
- ½ pound mushrooms, sliced

Pluck watercress leaves from stems and lightly pack in a measuring cup. Coarsely chop thinnest stems and add to leaves; discard thick stems. You should have about 4 cups lightly packed watercress.

Prepare Cooking Sauce and set aside. Sprinkle chicken chunks evenly with garlic, pepper, and ginger; set aside.

Place a wok over medium heat. When wok is hot, add sesame seeds (if used) and stir until golden (about 2 minutes); pour out of wok and set aside.

Increase heat to high; pour 2 tablespoons of the oil into wok. When oil is hot, add half the chicken and stir-fry until no longer pink in center; cut to test (about 3 minutes). Remove chicken from wok and set aside. Repeat to cook remaining chicken, using 1 tablespoon more oil.

Pour remaining 2 tablespoons oil into wok. When oil is hot, add mushrooms and stir-fry for about 3 minutes. Add watercress and toasted sesame seeds (if used); stir-fry for about 30 seconds.

Add chicken; stir Cooking Sauce and add. Stir until sauce boils and thickens. Makes 3 or 4 servings.

Cooking Sauce. Stir together 1 teaspoon *each* **corn-starch** and firmly packed **brown sugar,** 1 tablespoon **dry sherry,** and 2½ tablespoons **soy sauce.**

Per serving: 351 calories, 38 g protein, 7 g carbohydrates, 19 g total fat, 86 mg cholesterol, 764 mg sodium

---

Note: Recipes may be prepared in either a skillet or a wok.

(Pictured on facing page)

Chicken & Snow Peas

Preparation time: About 20 minutes, plus 30 minutes to soak mushrooms

Marinating time: About 15 minutes

Cooking time: About 10 minutes

Use either thin, flat Chinese pea pods (often sold as snow or sugar peas) or the thicker, crisper sugar snap peas in this classic Cantonese dish.

> 4 **dried Oriental mushrooms**
> 2 **teaspoons** *each* **soy sauce, cornstarch, dry sherry, and water**
> **Dash of white pepper**
> 1½ **pounds chicken breasts, skinned, boned, and cut into bite-size pieces**
> 3½ **tablespoons salad oil**
> **Cooking Sauce (recipe follows)**
> 1 **small clove garlic, minced or pressed**
> ½ **cup sliced bamboo shoots**
> ¼ **pound Chinese pea pods (also called snow or sugar peas) or sugar snap peas, ends and strings removed; or 1 package (6 oz.) frozen Chinese pea pods, thawed and drained**

Soak mushrooms in warm water to cover for 30 minutes, then drain. Cut off and discard stems; squeeze caps dry, thinly slice, and set aside.

In a bowl, mix soy, cornstarch, sherry, water, and white pepper. Add chicken and stir to coat, then stir in 1½ teaspoons of the oil. Let marinate for 15 minutes. Prepare Cooking Sauce; set aside.

Place a wok over high heat; when wok is hot, add 1 tablespoon of the oil. When oil begins to heat, add garlic and stir once. Add half the chicken mixture and stir-fry until meat is no longer pink in center; cut to test (about 3 minutes). Remove chicken from wok and set aside. Repeat to cook remaining chicken, adding 1 tablespoon more oil.

Pour remaining 1 tablespoon oil into wok. When oil is hot, add mushrooms and bamboo shoots. Stir-fry for 1 minute, adding a few drops of water if wok appears dry. Add pea pods and stir-fry for 3 minutes (30 seconds if using frozen pea pods), adding a few drops more water if wok appears dry. Return chicken to wok. Stir Cooking Sauce, pour into wok, and stir until sauce boils and thickens. Makes 3 or 4 servings.

Cooking Sauce. Stir together ½ cup **water,** 1 tablespoon **dry sherry,** 2 tablespoons **oyster sauce** or soy sauce, ¼ teaspoon **sugar,** 1 teaspoon **sesame oil,** and 1 tablespoon **cornstarch.**

Per serving: 294 calories, 28 g protein, 12 g carbohydrates, 15 g total fat, 65 mg cholesterol, 604 mg sodium

Almond Chicken

Follow directions for **Chicken & Snow Peas,** but first place wok over medium heat; when wok is hot, add 1 tablespoon **salad oil.** When oil is hot, add ½ cup **blanched almonds** and stir until golden (about 2 minutes); remove from wok and set aside. Stir in almonds just before serving.

Fruited Chicken Stir-fry

Preparation time: About 15 minutes

Cooking time: About 15 minutes

Slices of plum compete for attention with the chicken and vegetables in this tempting dish. The sweet-sour sauce is a bit out of the ordinary; it's based on peach nectar and lemon juice rather than the usual pineapple juice and vinegar.

> **Cooking Sauce (recipe follows)**
> 3 **medium-size firm-ripe Santa Rosa-type plums**
> 3 **to 4 tablespoons salad oil**
> 2 **teaspoons minced fresh ginger**
> 2 **whole chicken breasts (about 1 lb.** *each***), skinned, boned, and cut into ½- by 2-inch strips**
> 1 **large green bell pepper, seeded and cut into 1-inch squares**
> 1 **medium-size onion, cut into 1-inch cubes**

Prepare Cooking Sauce and set aside. Halve and pit plums; cut each half into ½-inch-thick wedges. Set aside.

Place a wok over high heat; when wok is hot, add 2 tablespoons of the oil. When oil is hot, add ginger and half the chicken. Stir-fry until meat is no longer pink in center; cut to test (about 3 minutes). Remove from wok and set aside. Repeat to cook remaining chicken, adding 1 tablespoon more oil if needed.

Pour remaining 1 tablespoon oil into wok. When oil is hot, add bell pepper and onion and stir-fry until tender-crisp to bite (about 4 minutes). Remove from wok. Add plums; stir-fry until softened (about 2 minutes). Stir sauce, pour into wok, and stir until boiling. Add chicken, bell pepper, and onion; stir until hot. Makes 4 servings.

Cooking Sauce. Stir together 1 cup **peach nectar,** ¼ cup **lemon juice,** 1 tablespoon **cornstarch,** 2 tablespoons **soy sauce,** and ½ teaspoon *each* **dry mustard** and crushed **anise seeds.**

Per serving: 345 calories, 36 g protein, 22 g carbohydrates, 13 g total fat, 86 mg cholesterol, 619 mg sodium

Once wok and ingredients are ready, it takes just minutes
to produce tantalizing Chicken & Snow Peas (recipe on facing page).
Crisp, emerald green pea pods share the spotlight with velvety
mushrooms and juicy chicken.

Chicken Pocket Sandwiches

Preparation time: About 10 minutes

Cooking time: About 15 minutes

A garlicky mixture of diced chicken breast, anchovies, and ripe olives makes a delicious stuffing for pocket breads—or for hollowed-out crusty rolls, if you like.

- 1 to 2 tablespoons salad oil
- 1 to 2 tablespoons butter or margarine
- 2 cloves garlic, minced or pressed
- ¼ to ½ teaspoon crushed red pepper
- 2 whole chicken breasts (about 1 lb. *each*), skinned, boned, and cut into ½-inch chunks
- 3 tablespoons *each* chopped parsley and drained, chopped capers
- 3 or 4 anchovy fillets, finely chopped
- 1 can (2¼ oz.) sliced ripe olives, drained
- ½ cup dry red wine
  Salt and black pepper
- 4 pocket breads, halved crosswise

Place a wok over medium-high heat. When wok is hot, add 1 tablespoon *each* of the oil and butter. When butter is melted, add garlic, red pepper, and half the chicken. Stir-fry until chicken is no longer pink in center; cut to test (about 3 minutes). Remove from wok and set aside; repeat to cook remaining chicken, adding more oil and butter as needed.

Return all chicken to wok. Stir in parsley, capers, anchovies, olives, and wine. Cook, stirring occasionally, until almost all liquid has evaporated (about 5 minutes). Season to taste with salt and black pepper.

Fill each bread half with an eighth of the chicken mixture. Makes about 4 servings.

Per serving: 434 calories, 41 g protein, 38 g carbohydrates, 12 g total fat, 96 mg cholesterol, 808 mg sodium

Kung Pao Chicken

Preparation time: About 10 minutes

Marinating time: 15 minutes

Cooking time: About 10 minutes

If you're fond of Chinese food and fiery flavors, you're almost certain to enjoy this Szechwan specialty. Chinese chefs often leave the charred whole chiles in the dish, but you can remove them if you prefer.

- 1 tablespoon *each* dry sherry and cornstarch
- ½ teaspoon salt
- ⅛ teaspoon white pepper
- 1½ pounds chicken breasts, skinned, boned, and cut into ½-inch chunks
- ¼ cup salad oil
  Cooking Sauce (recipe follows)
- 4 to 6 small dried hot red chiles
- ½ cup salted peanuts
- 1 teaspoon *each* minced garlic and grated fresh ginger
- 2 green onions (including tops), cut into 1½-inch lengths

In a bowl, stir together sherry, cornstarch, salt, and white pepper. Add chicken and stir to coat, then stir in 1 tablespoon of the oil and let marinate for 15 minutes. Meanwhile, prepare Cooking Sauce and set aside.

Place a wok over medium heat; when wok is hot, add 1 tablespoon of the oil. When oil is hot, add chiles and peanuts and stir until chiles just begin to char. (If chiles become completely black, discard them. Remove peanuts from wok and set aside; repeat with new oil and chiles.) Remove peanuts and chiles from wok; set aside.

Pour 1 tablespoon more oil into wok and increase heat to high. When oil begins to heat, add garlic and ginger and stir once, then add half the chicken mixture. Stir-fry until meat is no longer pink in center; cut to test (about 3 minutes). Remove from wok and set aside. Repeat to cook remaining chicken, adding remaining 1 tablespoon oil.

Return all chicken to wok; add peanuts, chiles, and onions. Stir Cooking Sauce and pour into wok; stir until sauce boils and thickens. Makes 4 servings.

Cooking Sauce. Stir together 2 tablespoons **soy sauce**, 1 tablespoon *each* **white wine vinegar** and **dry sherry**, 3 tablespoons **regular-strength chicken broth** or water, and 2 tablespoons *each* **sugar** and **cornstarch**.

Per serving: 425 calories, 32 g protein, 21 g carbohydrates, 25 g total fat, 65 mg cholesterol, 1,069 mg sodium

Chicken with Eggplant

Preparation time: About 15 minutes

Cooking time: About 20 minutes

The strips of chicken and eggplant are mild—but the sauce is spicy with dried chiles and grated fresh ginger. For even hotter flavor, add a few extra chiles.

- 1 **medium-size eggplant** (¾ to 1 lb.), cut into ¾- by 3-inch strips
  Boiling water
- 1 **tablespoon cornstarch**
- 2 **tablespoons soy sauce**
- 1 to 1¼ **pounds chicken breasts or thighs,** skinned, boned, and cut into ½- by 2-inch strips
- 6 **tablespoons salad oil**
- 1 or 2 **small dried hot red chiles,** split in half and seeded
- 1 **clove garlic,** minced or pressed
- 1 **teaspoon grated fresh ginger or** ½ teaspoon ground ginger
- ¼ **cup water**
- 1 **can** (about 8 oz.) **water chestnuts,** drained and sliced
- 3 **tablespoons regular-strength chicken broth or water**
- 1 **tablespoon dry sherry**
  Sliced green onions (including tops) or chopped parsley (optional)

Place eggplant in a bowl and pour boiling water over it to cover. Let stand for about 7 minutes; then drain and pat dry.

In another bowl, stir together cornstarch and soy; add chicken and stir to coat. Set aside.

Place a wok over high heat; when wok is hot, add ¼ cup of the oil. When oil is hot, add chiles. When chiles begin to brown, remove them from wok with a wire skimmer and discard them. Add garlic, ginger, eggplant, and 2 tablespoons of the water to wok; stir-fry for about 2 minutes. Add remaining 2 tablespoons water, cover, and cook, stirring frequently, until eggplant is tender when pierced (about 10 minutes). Remove from wok.

Pour remaining 2 tablespoons oil into wok; when oil is hot, add chicken mixture and water chestnuts. Stir-fry until meat is no longer pink in center; cut to test (about 3 to 5 minutes). Add broth, sherry, and eggplant mixture; cook for about 1 minute. Sprinkle with onions, if desired. Makes about 3 servings.

Per serving: 387 calories, 31 g protein, 21 g carbohydrates, 20 g total fat, 71 mg cholesterol, 856 mg sodium

Thai Chicken & Basil Stir-fry

Preparation time: 10 to 15 minutes, plus 30 minutes to soak mushrooms

Cooking time: About 15 minutes

An unusual combination of coconut milk, aromatic fish sauce, and fresh basil enhances chicken strips and succulent mushrooms. When you buy fish sauce, look for the Thai variety, labeled *nam pla;* the Vietnamese version, *nuoc mam,* is somewhat stronger-tasting.

- 6 **dried Oriental mushrooms,** *each* 2 to 3 inches in diameter
  Cooking Sauce (recipe follows)
- 2 to 3 **tablespoons salad oil**
- 1 **medium-size onion,** thinly sliced
- 3 **cloves garlic,** minced or pressed
- 2 **tablespoons minced fresh ginger**
- 2 **pounds chicken breasts,** skinned, boned, and cut into ¼-inch-wide strips
- 1½ **cups lightly packed slivered fresh basil leaves**
- 5 **green onions** (including tops), cut into 1-inch lengths

Soak mushrooms in warm water to cover for 30 minutes, then drain. Cut off and discard stems; squeeze caps dry, cut into ¼-inch slivers, and set aside.

Prepare Cooking Sauce and set aside.

Place a wok over high heat; when wok is hot, add 2 tablespoons of the oil. When oil is hot, add sliced onion, garlic, and ginger; stir-fry until onion is soft (about 4 minutes). Remove vegetables from wok and set aside.

Add half the chicken to wok and stir-fry until meat is tinged with brown (about 3 minutes). Remove from wok; set aside with cooked onion mixture. Repeat to brown remaining chicken, adding 1 tablespoon more oil if needed.

Pour Cooking Sauce into wok and boil until reduced by a third. Return onion mixture and chicken to wok. Add basil, mushrooms, and green onions; stir to heat through. Makes 4 or 5 servings.

Cooking Sauce. Stir together ¾ cup **canned or thawed frozen coconut milk,** 3 tablespoons *each* **soy sauce** and **rice wine vinegar,** 1½ tablespoons **fish sauce** (*nam pla*) or soy sauce, and ½ to 1 teaspoon **crushed dried hot red chiles.**

Per serving: 321 calories, 31 g protein, 12 g carbohydrates, 17 g total fat, 68 mg cholesterol, 1,011 mg sodium

Note: Recipes may be prepared in either a skillet or a wok.

Spread a little hoisin sauce on a crisp lettuce leaf, add a topping of hot,
savory chicken and vegetables—then wrap up and eat out of hand.
Egg rolls and grapes are good tasting accompaniments for Minced Chicken
in Lettuce (recipe on facing page).

(Pictured on facing page)

Minced Chicken in Lettuce

Preparation time: About 15 minutes, plus 30 minutes to soak mushrooms

Marinating time: 15 minutes

Cooking time: About 10 minutes

For an informal meal, serve minced chicken, mushrooms, bamboo shoots, and water chestnuts to wrap in chilled lettuce leaves and eat out of hand. Because there's not much sauce in the chicken mixture—just enough to hold the ingredients together—the lettuce stays crisp.

- 8 **medium-size dried Oriental mushrooms**
- 1 **teaspoon** *each* **cornstarch and soy sauce**
- 2 **teaspoons** *each* **dry sherry and water**
- ½ **teaspoon salt**
  Dash of white pepper
- 1½ **pounds chicken breasts, skinned, boned, and minced**
- ¼ **cup salad oil**
  Cooking Sauce (recipe follows)
- 1 **teaspoon minced fresh ginger**
- 2 **cloves garlic, minced**
- 2 **green onions (white part only), minced**
- 1 **can (about 8 oz.) sliced bamboo shoots, drained and minced**
- 1 **can (about 8 oz.) water chestnuts, drained and minced**
  Hoisin sauce ·
  About 30 iceberg lettuce leaves, chilled

Soak mushrooms in warm water to cover for 30 minutes, then drain. Cut off and discard stems; squeeze caps dry, mince, and set aside.

In a bowl, stir together cornstarch, soy, sherry, water, salt, and white pepper. Add chicken and stir to coat, then stir in 1½ teaspoons of the oil and let marinate for 15 minutes. Meanwhile, prepare Cooking Sauce and set aside.

Place a wok over high heat; when wok is hot, add 2 tablespoons of the oil. When oil is hot, add chicken and stir-fry until no longer pink (about 3 minutes). Remove from wok and set aside.

Pour remaining 1½ tablespoons oil into wok. When oil begins to heat, add ginger, garlic, and onions and stir once. Then add mushrooms, bamboo shoots, and water chestnuts and stir-fry for 2 minutes. Return chicken to wok. Stir Cooking Sauce, pour into wok, and stir until sauce boils and thickens.

To eat, spread a little hoisin on a lettuce leaf, top with some of the hot chicken mixture, and fold lettuce to enclose; eat out of hand. Makes 4 to 6 servings.

Cooking Sauce. Stir together 1 teaspoon **soy sauce,** 1 tablespoon **dry sherry,** 2 tablespoons *each* **oyster sauce** and **water,** 1 teaspoon **sesame oil,** ½ teaspoon **sugar,** and 2 teaspoons **cornstarch.**

Per serving: 225 calories, 19 g protein, 13 g carbohydrates, 11 g total fat, 43 mg cholesterol, 601 mg sodium

Many-spice Chicken

Preparation time: About 10 minutes

Cooking time: About 5 minutes

The distinctive flavor of this stir-fry comes from anise-flavored liqueur and a seasoning blend of eight dried herbs and spices. The liqueur is readily available in liquor stores; you'll find it sold under several names, including *ouzo* and *pastis* (avoid the syrupy cordial anisette). If you don't enjoy the licoricelike taste of anise, use dry sherry in place of liqueur; you'll end up with an equally good—though different—dish.

- ¼ **cup salad oil**
- 2 **tablespoons anise-flavored liqueur or dry sherry**
- 2 **tablespoons minced fresh ginger**
- 1 **teaspoon** *each* **minced garlic and soy sauce**
- 3 **tablespoons thinly sliced green onions (including tops)**
- ¼ **teaspoon** *each* **dry mustard, chili powder, pepper, dry oregano leaves, dry sage leaves, dry thyme leaves, ground cloves, and ground cinnamon**
- ¼ **teaspoon** *each* **salt, sugar, and all-purpose flour**
- 1 **whole chicken breast (about 1 lb.), skinned, boned, and cut into bite-size pieces**
  Chopped parsley

In a small bowl, stir together 2 tablespoons of the oil, liqueur, ginger, garlic, soy, onions, mustard, chili powder, pepper, oregano, sage, thyme, cloves, cinnamon, salt, sugar, and flour. Set aside.

Place a wok over high heat; when wok is hot, add remaining 2 tablespoons oil. When oil is hot, add chicken and stir-fry until meat is no longer pink in center; cut to test (about 3 minutes). Add liqueur mixture and stir constantly until mixture boils and thickens (about 1 minute). Sprinkle with parsley. Makes 2 servings.

Per serving: 479 calories, 35 g protein, 9 g carbohydrates, 29 g total fat, 86 mg cholesterol, 543 mg sodium

Note: Recipes may be prepared in either a skillet or a wok.

Chicken with Two-tone Pears

Preparation time: About 15 minutes

Cooking time: About 15 minutes

Slices of golden- and red-skinned pears add an especially handsome touch to this dish. If you can't find red pears, just use two yellow ones—but in any case, look for richly fragrant fruit with flesh that's tender but still slightly firm to the touch.

> Cooking Sauce (recipe follows)
> 3 tablespoons salad oil
> 2 cloves garlic, minced or pressed
> 2 whole chicken breasts (about 1 lb. *each*), skinned, boned, and cut into bite-size pieces
> 2 stalks celery, thinly sliced
> 3 green onions (including tops), cut into 2-inch lengths
> 1 can (about 8 oz.) sliced bamboo shoots, drained
> ¼ pound Chinese pea pods (also called snow or sugar peas) or sugar snap peas, ends and strings removed; or 1 package (6 oz.) frozen Chinese pea pods, thawed and drained
> 1 *each* small red and yellow pear, quartered, cored, and cut into ½-inch-thick slices
> Salt
> ½ cup salted roasted cashews

Prepare Cooking Sauce and set aside.

Place a wok over high heat; when wok is hot, add 1 tablespoon of the oil. When oil is hot, add garlic and half the chicken. Stir-fry until chicken is no longer pink in center; cut to test (about 3 minutes). Remove from wok and set aside. Repeat to cook remaining chicken, adding 1 tablespoon more oil.

Pour remaining 1 tablespoon oil into wok. When oil is hot, add celery, onions, and bamboo shoots; stir-fry for about 1 minute. Add pea pods and stir-fry for 3 minutes (30 seconds if using frozen pea pods), adding a few drops of water if wok appears dry. Add pears and chicken; stir Cooking Sauce and add. Stir until sauce boils and thickens. Season to taste with salt; garnish with cashews. Makes 6 servings.

Cooking Sauce. Stir together 4 teaspoons **cornstarch,** 1 teaspoon **sugar,** 2 teaspoons minced **fresh ginger,** 2 tablespoons *each* **soy sauce** and **dry sherry,** and ¾ cup **regular-strength chicken broth.**

Per serving: 297 calories, 27 g protein, 17 g carbohydrates, 14 g total fat, 57 mg cholesterol, 616 mg sodium

Chicken & Garlic Stir-fry

Preparation time: About 45 minutes

Chilling time for pickles: At least 1 day

Cooking time: About 5 minutes

Pickled garlic or shallots add sparkle to this dish. You'll need to make the pickles at least a day in advance (or up to 2 months ahead, if you like), but actual cooking time is extra-short—just 5 minutes.

Our pickle recipe yields 3 cups—more than you'll need for this stir-fry. Try using leftover pickles in salads; the liquid is good in dressings.

> ⅓ cup Garlic or Shallot Pickles (recipe follows), drained
> Cooking Sauce (recipe follows)
> 2 tablespoons salad oil
> 1 whole chicken breast (about 1 lb.), skinned, boned, and cut into ¼- by 3-inch strips
> 4 green onions (including tops), cut into 2-inch lengths

At least 1 day ahead prepare Garlic or Shallot Pickles and refrigerate.

Prepare Cooking Sauce and set aside.

Place a wok over high heat; when wok is hot, add oil. When oil is hot, add chicken and stir-fry until lightly browned (about 2 minutes). Add onions; then stir Cooking Sauce and add. Continue to stir until sauce boils and thickens. Stir in pickles. Serve immediately. Makes 3 servings.

Garlic or Shallot Pickles. Peel 3 cups (about 1 lb.) **garlic** cloves or small shallots. Cut any garlic cloves or shallots that are thicker than ¾ inch in half lengthwise.

In a 2- to 3-quart pan, combine 1½ cups **distilled white vinegar,** ⅓ cup **sugar,** and ½ teaspoon **salt.**

Bring to a boil over high heat, stirring until sugar is dissolved. Drop garlic into boiling vinegar mixture and cook, uncovered, stirring occasionally, for 1 minute. Let cool.

Place pickles and their liquid in a jar, cover tightly, and refrigerate for at least 1 day or for up to 2 months. Makes about 3 cups.

Cooking Sauce. Stir together ½ cup **regular-strength chicken broth,** 2 teaspoons **cornstarch,** and 1 table-spoon *each* **soy sauce** and **liquid from garlic pickles.**

Per serving: 324 calories, 27 g protein, 32 g carbohydrates, 11 g total fat, 57 mg cholesterol, 236 mg sodium

Cashew Chicken

Preparation time: About 15 minutes

Cooking time: About 8 minutes

Cashew chicken is adaptable—you can use peanuts, almonds, or walnut halves in place of the cashews, or substitute another favorite vegetable for the bell pepper.

 Cooking Sauce (recipe follows)
1 tablespoon soy sauce
1 teaspoon cornstarch
1 whole chicken breast (about 1 lb.), skinned, boned, and cut into bite-size pieces
3 tablespoons salad oil
½ cup salted roasted cashews
1 medium-size green bell pepper, seeded and cut into 1-inch squares
1 medium-size onion, cut into 8 wedges, layers separated
½ teaspoon finely minced fresh ginger or ¼ teaspoon ground ginger

Prepare Cooking Sauce and set aside. In a bowl, stir together soy and cornstarch; add chicken and stir to coat. Set aside.

Place a wok over medium-high heat; when wok is hot, add 2 tablespoons of the oil. When oil is hot, add cashews and stir until browned (about 1 minute). Remove with a slotted spoon and set aside. Add chicken mixture and stir-fry until meat is no longer pink in center; cut to test (about 3 minutes). Remove from wok and set aside.

Pour remaining 1 tablespoon oil into wok; when oil is hot, add bell pepper, onion, and ginger and stir-fry until pepper is tender-crisp to bite (about 4 minutes). Return chicken to wok. Stir Cooking Sauce and pour into wok; stir until sauce boils and thickens. Stir in cashews. Makes 2 servings.

Cooking Sauce. Stir together ½ teaspoon **cornstarch,** a dash of **liquid hot pepper seasoning,** ¾ teaspoon *each* **sugar** and **white wine vinegar,** 1 teaspoon **dry sherry** or water, and 1 tablespoon **soy sauce.**

Per serving: 579 calories, 42 g protein, 19 g carbohydrates, 38 g total fat, 86 mg cholesterol, 1,335 mg sodium

Coq au Vin Sauté

Preparation time: About 15 minutes

Cooking time: About 25 minutes

Here's a quick and easy adaptation of a classic French dish. The robust sauce is flavored with red wine and Dijon mustard.

1 tablespoon salad oil
⅓ pound lean boneless pork (such as shoulder or butt), trimmed of excess fat and cut into ½-inch cubes
2 whole chicken breasts (about 1 lb. *each*), skinned, boned, and cut into ½- by 2-inch strips
1 large onion, finely chopped
½ pound small mushrooms, thinly sliced
1 can (14½ oz.) regular-strength chicken broth
1 cup dry red wine
2 tablespoons Dijon mustard
1 teaspoon *each* cornstarch and water, stirred together
2 tablespoons chopped parsley

Place a wok over medium-high heat; when wok is hot, add oil. When oil is hot, add pork and stir-fry until well browned (about 7 minutes). Lift out meat and set aside; leave drippings in wok.

Add half the chicken to wok. Stir-fry until meat is no longer pink in center; cut to test (3 to 4 minutes). Remove from wok and set aside. Repeat to cook remaining chicken.

Increase heat to high. Add onion and mush-rooms; stir-fry until onion is soft (about 3 minutes). Remove vegetables from wok and set aside. Pour broth into wok, bring to a boil, and boil until reduced to 1 cup. Stir in wine and mustard and bring to a boil. Add pork, reduce heat, and simmer for 5 minutes.

Return chicken and vegetables to wok along with cornstarch-water mixture. Bring to a boil, stir-ring until slightly thickened. Sprinkle with parsley. Makes about 4 servings.

Per serving: 314 calories, 44 g protein, 9 g carbohydrates, 11 g total fat, 111 mg cholesterol, 806 mg sodium

Note: Recipes may be prepared in either a skillet or a wok.

(Pictured on facing page)

Chicken in Tomato Sauce

Preparation time: About 15 minutes

Cooking time: About 30 minutes

Cut into 2-inch chunks, chicken cooks quickly in a rich, brandied tomato sauce. Serve on a bed of zucchini sticks (just follow directions for Zucchini Sticks on page 92, cutting zucchini into noodle-thin strips).

To make easy work of cutting the chicken, use a well-sharpened heavy knife or cleaver.

> 1 frying chicken (3 to 3½ lbs.), cut up
> 2 tablespoons salad oil
> Salt and pepper
> 2 tablespoons brandy
> 1 small onion, finely chopped
> ¼ pound mushrooms, sliced
> 1 fresh rosemary sprig (2 to 3 inches long) or 1 teaspoon dry rosemary
> 1 tablespoon all-purpose flour
> ½ cup dry white wine
> 1 can (about 14 oz.) pear-shaped tomatoes
> Fresh rosemary sprigs (optional)

Pull off and discard all visible fat from chicken pieces, then rinse chicken and pat dry. With a heavy knife or cleaver, cut each chicken piece through bones into 2-inch lengths.

Place a wok over medium-high heat; when wok is hot, add oil. When oil is hot, add thickest dark-meat pieces of chicken and cook, turning, until browned on both sides (about 5 minutes). Add remaining chicken. Continue to cook, turning, until pieces are well browned on both sides and meat near thighbone is no longer pink; cut to test (about 15 more minutes). Season to taste with salt and pepper.

Add brandy; when liquid bubbles, carefully ignite (not beneath an exhaust fan or near flammable items), then shake wok until flames die down. Lift out chicken pieces. Spoon off and discard all but about 1 tablespoon of the drippings.

Add onion, mushrooms, and 1 rosemary sprig (or 1 teaspoon dry rosemary) to drippings in wok; stir-fry until onion is soft (about 4 minutes). Sprinkle in flour and stir until golden. Blend in wine and bring to a boil. Add tomatoes (break up with a spoon) and their liquid; bring to a simmer. Return chicken to wok and stir gently just until heated through. Garnish with rosemary, if desired. Makes 4 servings.

Per serving: 518 calories, 50 g protein, 8 g carbohydrates, 31 g total fat, 154 mg cholesterol, 308 mg sodium

Cuban Chicken

Preparation time: About 15 minutes

Cooking time: About 1 hour

Raisins, olives, and chopped peppers join chicken pieces and potato chunks in this colorful stew. You may accompany chicken and sauce with Orange-scented Rice and a crisp salad.

> 1 frying chicken (3 to 3½ lbs.), cut up
> 2 tablespoons salad oil
> 2 cloves garlic, minced or pressed
> 1 large onion, chopped
> 1 large green bell pepper, seeded and chopped
> 4 small thin-skinned potatoes, cut into 1-inch chunks
> ¾ teaspoon *each* dry oregano leaves and ground cumin
> 1 can (15 oz.) tomato sauce
> ⅓ cup dry white wine
> ½ cup *each* raisins and pitted ripe olives
> Orange-scented Rice (recipe follows), optional
> 1 cup frozen peas, thawed and drained

Rinse chicken and pat dry. Place a wok over medium-high heat; when wok is hot, add oil. When oil is hot, add half the chicken pieces; cook, turning, until browned on all sides (about 15 minutes). Remove from wok and set aside. Repeat to brown remaining chicken. Spoon off and discard all but 2 tablespoons of the drippings.

Add garlic, onion, and bell pepper to drippings in wok. Stir-fry until onion is soft (about 4 minutes). Add potatoes, oregano, cumin, tomato sauce, wine, raisins, olives, and chicken. Bring to a boil. Then reduce heat, cover, and simmer, turning chicken once, until meat near thighbone is no longer pink; cut to test (about 35 minutes). Meanwhile, prepare Orange-scented Rice and keep warm.

Skim and discard fat from chicken stew, then stir in peas and cook just until hot. Accompany chicken and sauce with Orange-scented Rice, if desired. Makes about 4 servings.

Orange-scented Rice. In a 2-quart pan, combine 1 cup *each* **regular-strength chicken broth** and **fresh orange juice;** stir in grated **peel of 1 orange.** Bring to a boil; add 1 cup **long-grain white rice,** stir once, and reduce heat to low. Cover and simmer until liquid is absorbed (about 20 minutes).

Per serving: 727 calories, 55 g protein, 51 g carbohydrates, 35 g total fat, 154 mg cholesterol, 965 mg sodium

Note: Recipes may be prepared in either a skillet or a wok.

A rosemary sprig tops robust Italian-inspired Chicken in
Tomato Sauce (recipe on facing page). This speedy version of classic
chicken *cacciatore* can be ready in just half an hour. If you like,
serve it atop low-calorie zucchini instead of pasta.

Garlic Celebration Chicken

Preparation time: About 20 minutes

Cooking time: About 1¼ hours

Simmered in white wine and vermouth and seasoned with basil and plenty of garlic, this hearty entrée is a good choice for a cool-weather meal. Wedges of ripe tomato make a pretty, fresh-tasting garnish.

  1 **frying chicken (3 to 3½ lbs.), cut up**
  4 **slices bacon, chopped**
  2 **medium-size onions, chopped**
  5 **cloves garlic, minced or pressed**
  1 **cup dry white wine**
  ¼ **cup dry vermouth or dry white wine**
  1 **tablespoon dry basil**
  1 **teaspoon poultry seasoning**
     Salt and pepper
  1 **tablespoon** *each* **cornstarch and water, stirred together**
  2 **medium-size tomatoes, cut into wedges**

Rinse chicken and pat dry; set aside.

Place a wok over medium-high heat; when wok is hot, add bacon and stir-fry until crisp (about 2 minutes). Lift out bacon with a slotted spoon, leaving drippings in wok; drain bacon and set aside.

Add half the chicken to wok; cook, turning, until browned on all sides (about 15 minutes). Remove from wok and set aside. Repeat to brown remaining chicken.

Add onions and garlic to wok and stir-fry until onions are soft (about 4 minutes). Spoon off and discard any fat from wok; add wine, vermouth, basil, poultry seasoning, bacon, and chicken pieces. Bring

to a boil over high heat. Then reduce heat, cover, and simmer, turning once, until meat near thighbone is no longer pink; cut to test (about 35 minutes).

Arrange chicken on a platter; keep warm. Skim and discard fat from pan juices, then season to taste with salt and pepper. Stir cornstarch-water mixture into pan juices; continue to stir until sauce is thickened. Garnish chicken with tomatoes; pass sauce at the table. Makes about 4 servings.

Per serving: 505 calories, 51 g protein, 12 g carbohydrates, 27 g total fat, 159 mg cholesterol, 256 mg sodium

Fragrant Braised Chicken

Preparation time: About 5 minutes

Cooking time: About 1 hour

This chicken is braised in a broth seasoned with cumin, cardamom, cinnamon, and pepper, spices familiar to Indian-style cooking. Garnish it with juicy orange slices and sprigs of fresh cilantro.

     Seasoned Broth (recipe follows)
  1 **frying chicken (3 to 3½ lbs.), skinned and cup up**
     Pepper
  3 **tablespoons salad oil**
  2 **dry bay leaves**
  1 **cinnamon stick (about 3 inches long)**
  6 **whole cloves**
  5 **whole black peppercorns**
  3 **cloves garlic, minced or pressed**
     Orange slices
     Fresh cilantro (coriander) sprigs

Prepare Seasoned Broth and set aside.

Rinse chicken, pat dry, and sprinkle lightly with pepper.

Place a wok over medium-high heat; when wok is hot, add oil. When oil is hot, add bay leaves, cinnamon stick, cloves, and peppercorns; then add half the chicken and cook, uncovered, turning occasionally, until browned on all sides (about 10 minutes). Remove from wok and set aside. Repeat to brown remaining chicken.

Return all chicken to wok. Stir in Seasoned Broth and garlic; bring to a boil. Then reduce heat, cover, and simmer, turning chicken once, until meat near thighbone is no longer pink; cut to test (about 35 minutes).

Transfer chicken to a serving dish. Skim and discard any fat from pan juices; pour juices over chicken. Garnish with orange slices and cilantro. Makes about 4 servings.

Seasoned Broth. In a bowl, combine 1 cup **regular-strength chicken broth**, 2 teaspoons *each* **soy sauce** and **Worcestershire**, 1 teaspoon **ground cumin**, ¼ teaspoon **ground red pepper** (cayenne), and ⅛ teaspoon **ground cardamom**.

Per serving: 530 calories, 49 g protein, 3 g carbohydrates, 35 g total fat, 154 mg cholesterol, 596 mg sodium

Turkey Chili

Preparation time: About 15 minutes

Cooking time: About 45 minutes

An alternative to traditional beef chili is this version made with chunks of turkey. At the table, offer lime wedges, cheese, chopped tomato, and green onions to embellish individual servings.

   2 **tablespoons salad oil**
   1 **onion, chopped**
   1 **small green bell pepper, seeded and chopped**
   1 **clove garlic, minced or pressed**
   1½ **pounds turkey breast, skinned, boned, and cut into bite-size chunks**
   1 **small can (about 8 oz.) tomatoes, drained and chopped**
   2 **cans (about 15 oz.** *each***) kidney beans, drained**
   1 **can (15 oz.) tomato sauce**
   2 **tablespoons soy sauce**
   1½ **tablespoons chili powder**
   ½ **teaspoon** *each* **ground cumin, dry sage leaves, and dry thyme leaves**
      Garnishes (suggestions follow)

Place a wok over medium-high heat; when wok is hot, add oil. When oil is hot, add onion, bell pepper, and garlic; stir-fry until onion is soft (about 4 minutes). Remove from wok and set aside.

Increase heat to high. Add half the turkey and stir-fry until no longer pink in center; cut to test (about 3 minutes). Remove from wok and set aside. Repeat to cook remaining turkey.

Return all turkey and vegetables to wok. Then add tomatoes, beans, tomato sauce, soy, chili powder, cumin, sage, and thyme. Bring to a boil; reduce heat, cover, and simmer until chili is thick and flavors are well blended (about 30 minutes; uncover for last 5 minutes).

To serve, ladle hot chili into bowls; offer garnishes to embellish individual servings. Makes 4 servings.

Garnishes. Offer **lime wedges,** sliced **green onions** (including tops), shredded **jack or Cheddar cheese,** and chopped **tomatoes.**

Per serving: 476 calories, 47 g protein, 50 g carbohydrates, 11 g total fat, 84 mg cholesterol, 2,074 mg sodium

Turkey & Green Bean Stir-fry

Preparation time: About 15 minutes

Cooking time: About 15 minutes

Readily available turkey breast is a nice alternative to chicken in stir-fry dishes; though not as velvety-textured as chicken, it's every bit as tasty. This easy-to-prepare dish features turkey with fresh green beans and celery; if you like, offer toasted almonds or sesame seeds to sprinkle on top.

      Cooking Sauce (recipe follows)
   1 **egg white**
   2 **tablespoons soy sauce**
   2 **pounds turkey breast, skinned, boned, and cut into ¼- by 2-inch strips**
   ¼ **cup salad oil**
   ½ **pound green beans (ends removed), cut into 2-inch pieces**
   ½ **cup thinly sliced celery**
   ½ **cup thinly sliced onion, separated into rings**
   6 **tablespoons water or dry sherry**
   1 **or 2 cloves garlic, minced or pressed**

Prepare Cooking Sauce; set aside.

In a bowl, beat together egg white and soy; add turkey and stir to coat. Set aside. Place a wok over high heat; when wok is hot, add 2 tablespoons of the oil. When oil is hot, add beans, celery, and onion; stir-fry for about 1 minute, then add water. Cover and cook, stirring occasionally, until beans are tender-crisp to bite (about 4 minutes).

Remove vegetables from wok, then add remaining 2 tablespoons oil. When oil is hot, add garlic and half the turkey. Stir-fry until meat is no longer pink in center; cut to test (about 3 minutes). Remove from wok. Repeat to cook remaining turkey; return all turkey to wok along with green bean mixture. Stir Cooking Sauce, pour into wok, and stir until sauce boils and thickens. Makes 4 servings.

Cooking Sauce. Mix 1 tablespoon *each* **cornstarch** and **soy sauce,** 2 tablespoons **dry sherry,** ½ teaspoon **ground ginger,** and ½ cup **water.**

Per serving: 376 calories, 45 g protein, 10 g carbohydrates, 17 g total fat, 111 mg cholesterol, 922 mg sodium

Note: Recipes may be prepared in either a skillet or a wok.

Ready in minutes from your wok, Sweet & Sour Fish
(recipe on facing page) is a seafood lover's symphony of contrasts.
Nuggets of fish, onion, green pepper, and tomato
harmonize in a tangy sauce.

Fish & Shellfish

(Pictured on facing page)
Sweet & Sour Fish

Preparation time: About 15 minutes

Cooking time: 12 minutes

Sweet-sour sauce is just as good with fish as it is with pork or chicken. Here, the familiar red sauce enhances a combination of bell pepper squares, tomato, and chunks of turbot or halibut.

    Sweet-Sour Sauce (recipe follows)
    About ⅓ cup cornstarch
2 **pounds turbot or halibut fillets, cut into ½-inch squares**
    About 6 tablespoons salad oil
1 **clove garlic, minced or pressed**
1 **onion, cut into 1-inch cubes**
1 **medium-size green bell pepper, seeded and cut into ½-inch thick strips**
1 **medium-size tomato, cut into 1-inch cubes**
    Fresh cilantro (coriander) or Italian parsley (optional)

Prepare Sweet-Sour Sauce and set aside.

Place cornstarch in a bag, add fish pieces, and shake to coat completely; shake off excess.

Place a wok over medium-high heat; when wok is hot, add 2 tablespoons of the oil. When oil is hot, add some of the fish; stir-fry until fish is browned on all sides and flakes when prodded (about 2 minutes). Remove from wok and keep warm. Repeat to cook remaining fish, adding about 2 tablespoons more oil.

Increase heat to high and pour 2 tablespoons more oil into wok. When oil is hot, add garlic, onion, and bell pepper; stir-fry for 2 minutes. Stir Sweet-Sour Sauce; pour into wok and stir in tomato. Bring to a boil, stirring. Return fish and any accumulated juices to wok; stir to combine. Garnish with cilantro, if desired. Makes 4 servings.

Sweet-Sour Sauce. Stir together 1 tablespoon **cornstarch** and ¼ cup **sugar.** Stir in 2 tablespoons *each* **soy sauce** and **catsup,** ¼ cup **distilled white vinegar,** and ½ cup **regular-strength chicken broth.**

Per serving: 736 calories, 35 g protein, 31 g carbohydrates, 52 g total fat, 104 mg cholesterol, 915 mg sodium

Lemony Fish with Asparagus

Preparation time: About 10 minutes

Cooking time: About 5 minutes

Bright green asparagus and delicate white-fleshed fish are flavored with fresh lemon in this simple and speedy entrée.

1 **pound asparagus**
2 **teaspoons *each* cornstarch, lemon juice, and salad oil**
¾ **pound orange roughy, sea bass, or halibut fillets, *each* about ½ inch thick, cut into 1- by 3-inch strips**
3 **tablespoons salad oil**
1 **large clove garlic, minced or pressed**
2 **tablespoons regular-strength chicken broth or water**
2 **tablespoons lemon juice**

Snap off and discard tough ends of asparagus; cut spears into ½-inch slanting slices. Set aside.

In a bowl, stir together cornstarch, the 2 teaspoons lemon juice, and the 2 teaspoons oil. Add fish and stir gently until evenly coated.

Place a wok over medium-high heat; when wok is hot, add 2 tablespoons of the oil. When oil is hot, add fish and stir-fry until opaque (about 2 minutes); remove fish from wok and set aside.

Pour remaining 1 tablespoon oil into wok. When oil begins to heat, add garlic and stir-fry for about 30 seconds. Then add asparagus and stir-fry for 1 minute. Stir together broth and the 2 tablespoons lemon juice; pour into wok, cover, and cook, stirring often, until asparagus is tender-crisp to bite (2 to 3 more minutes). Return fish and any accumulated juices to wok and stir just until heated through. Makes 3 or 4 servings.

Per serving: 199 calories, 16 g protein, 4 g carbohydrates, 13 g total fat, 40 mg cholesterol, 294 mg sodium

Lemony Fish with Fennel

Follow directions for **Lemony Fish with Asparagus,** but substitute 1 large **fennel** bulb for asparagus. To prepare fennel, trim off and discard stalks, reserving a few of the feathery leaves for garnish. Cut away and discard base; cut bulb in half lengthwise, then thinly slice crosswise. (Fennel may need to cook for a few more minutes than asparagus.) Garnish dish with reserved fennel leaves.

Note: Recipes may be prepared in either a skillet or a wok.

A Light Technique

Stir-frying is widely appreciated for its bright, fresh-tasting results. But not everyone realizes that those rich colors and peak flavors can be enjoyed for a surprisingly small investment of calories. The following hearty entrées, for example, weigh in at just 226 to 274 calories per serving.

If it's salt that you wish to reduce, use a low-sodium soy sauce. We also recommend using your own homemade unsalted chicken broth in these and other stir-fries; you and your guests can add salt to taste at the table.

Lamb with Spring Onions

- 1 **pound boneless leg of lamb**
- ½ **teaspoon Chinese five-spice**
- 1 **egg white**
- 2 **cloves garlic, slivered**
- 4 **thin, quarter-size slices fresh ginger or ⅛ teaspoon ground ginger**
- 1 **tablespoon cornstarch**
- 5 **teaspoons soy sauce**
- 6 **tablespoons dry sherry**
- 2 **tablespoons water**
- 10 **green onions (including tops)**
- 2 **tablespoons salad oil**

Trim and discard fat from lamb; cut meat into bite-size strips ⅛ inch thick. In a bowl, mix lamb, five-spice, egg white, garlic, ginger, 1 teaspoon of the cornstarch, and 1 teaspoon of the soy. Let stand for 10 minutes.

Meanwhile, blend sherry, water, remaining 2 teaspoons cornstarch, and remaining 4 teaspoons soy in a small bowl. Cut off white part of each onion, then cut each of these pieces in half. Cut two 1½-inch-long sections from each green top; discard remainder of green tops.

Place a wok over high heat; when wok is hot, add oil. When oil is hot, add meat mixture and stir-fry until lightly browned (2 to 3 minutes). Return to bowl.

To wok, add sherry mixture and white part of onions. Cook, stirring, until mixture is thickened. Add meat mixture and onion tops and cook, stirring, just until heated through (1 to 2 minutes). Makes 4 servings.

Per serving: 226 calories, 21 g protein, 8 g carbohydrates, 12 g total fat, 66 mg cholesterol, 511 mg sodium

Beef & Vegetable Sauté

- ⅓ **cup firmly packed brown sugar**
- 2 **tablespoons cornstarch**
- ¼ **cup cider vinegar**
- 3 **tablespoons soy sauce**
- 1½ **pounds top round or flank steak, cut ½ to ¾ inch thick**
- 2 **tablespoons butter or margarine**
- 1 **large onion, thinly sliced**
- 1½ **cups thinly sliced carrots**
- 1 **cup green beans, in 1-inch lengths**
- 1 **cup water**
- 1½ **cups thinly sliced zucchini**

In a small bowl, stir together sugar, cornstarch, vinegar, and soy until cornstarch is dissolved. Set aside.

Trim and discard fat from meat. Cut meat into slanting slices ⅛ to ¼ inch thick.

Place a wok over medium heat; when wok is hot, add 1 tablespoon of the butter. When butter is melted, add meat strips, a few at a time, and stir-fry until well browned, adding remaining 1 tablespoon butter as needed. As meat is browned, lift out and set aside.

When all meat has been cooked, add onion, carrots, beans, and ½ cup of the water to wok; stir well, cover, and cook, stirring often, for 8 minutes. Stir in zucchini and remaining ½ cup water; cook, uncovered, just until all vegetables are tender to bite (about 2 more minutes).

Stir cornstarch mixture and add to vegetables along with meat; stir until sauce boils and thickens. Serve immediately. Makes 6 servings.

Per serving: 274 calories, 26 g protein, 23 g carbohydrates, 9 g total fat, 71 mg cholesterol, 628 mg sodium

Shrimp with Peking Sauce

- **Peking Stir-fry Sauce (recipe follows)**
- 2 **tablespoons salad oil**
- 1 **pound medium-size raw shrimp, shelled and deveined**

1 large red onion, slivered

2 cups broccoli flowerets

1 red bell pepper, seeded and cut into long strips

1 green or yellow bell pepper, seeded and cut into long strips

2 to 4 tablespoons water

2 teaspoons cornstarch

Prepare Peking Stir-fry Sauce; set aside.

Place a wok over high heat; when wok is hot, add 1 tablespoon of the oil. When oil is hot, add shrimp. Stir-fry just until shrimp turn pink (about 2 minutes). Remove shrimp from wok.

Add remaining 1 tablespoon oil, onion, broccoli, all bell peppers, and 1 tablespoon of the water. Stir-fry, adding more water as needed, until broccoli is barely tender to bite (2 to 4 minutes).

Blend cornstarch into prepared sauce. Add to wok and stir just until sauce is thickened and clear. Add shrimp; stir just until heated through. Serve immediately. Makes 4 servings.

Peking Stir-fry Sauce. Stir together 2 cloves **garlic,** minced or pressed; 2 tablespoons minced **fresh ginger** or 1 teaspoon ground ginger; ½ cup **water;** ¼ cup **hoisin sauce;** 2 tablespoons **soy sauce;** 1 tablespoon **rice wine vinegar;** and 2 teaspoons **sugar.**

Per serving: 246 calories, 23 g protein, 19 g carbohydrates, 9 g total fat, 140 mg cholesterol, 1179 mg sodium

Asparagus Chicken Stir-fry

½ cup Homemade Chicken Broth (recipe follows) or regular-strength chicken broth

8 green onions (including tops)

1 pound asparagus

½ pound mushrooms

1 tablespoon *each* cornstarch, dry sherry, and soy sauce

3 tablespoons sesame oil or salad oil

1 tablespoon minced fresh ginger or ½ teaspoon ground ginger

2 cloves garlic, minced or pressed

1½ pounds chicken breasts, skinned, boned, and cut into ½- by 1-inch strips

Prepare Homemade Chicken Broth and set aside.

Cut onions diagonally into 1-inch pieces. Snap off and discard tough ends of asparagus; cut spears into 1-inch slanting slices. Thinly slice mushrooms. Combine cornstarch, sherry, soy, and broth; stir until cornstarch is dissolved.

Place a wok over high heat; when wok is hot, add oil. When oil is hot, add ginger, garlic, and chicken. Stir-fry until chicken is no longer pink in center; cut to test (about 2 minutes). Lift chicken from wok and set aside.

To wok, add onions, asparagus, and mushrooms; stir-fry for 1 minute. Add chicken; stir broth mixture and add. Bring to a boil, stirring; stir for 1 more minute. Makes 4 servings.

Per serving: 268 calories, 30 g protein, 10 g carbohydrates, 12 g total fat, 65 mg cholesterol, 343 mg sodium

Homemade Chicken Broth. Rinse 5 pounds **bony chicken pieces** (wings, backs, necks, carcasses); place in a 6- to 8-quart pan. Add 2 large **onions,** cut into chunks; 2 large **carrots,** cut into chunks; 6 to 8 **parsley sprigs;** ½ teaspoon **whole black peppercorns;** and 3½ quarts **water.** Bring to a boil; then reduce heat, cover, and simmer for 3 hours. Let cool.

Strain broth into a bowl. Discard scraps. Cover broth and refrigerate until fat solidifies (at least 4 hours)

or for up to 2 days. Lift off and discard fat. To store, freeze in 1-cup to 4-cup portions. Makes about 10 cups.

Vegetable & Bulgur Stir-fry

2 tablespoons salad oil

1 cup bulgur

1 tablespoon sesame seeds

2 medium-size carrots, thinly sliced

1 *each* medium-size zucchini and crookneck squash, thinly sliced

¼ pound mushrooms, thinly sliced

1 clove garlic, minced or pressed

½ teaspoon *each* dry basil, dry marjoram leaves, and dry oregano leaves

⅛ teaspoon pepper

1¾ cups water

2 cups broccoli flowerets

½ cup shredded jack cheese

½ cup sliced green onions (including tops)

3 pocket breads, halved and warmed (optional)

Lemon wedges

Place a wok over medium-high heat; when wok is hot, add 1 tablespoon of the oil. When oil is hot, add bulgur, sesame seeds, and carrots; stir-fry for 2 minutes. Add remaining 1 tablespoon oil, zucchini, crookneck squash, mushrooms, and garlic; stir-fry for 2 more minutes. Add herbs, pepper, and water; reduce heat, cover, and simmer until liquid is absorbed (about 10 minutes).

Add broccoli; cover and cook for 2 minutes. Stir in cheese. Sprinkle with onions and spoon into pocket bread, if desired. Serve with lemon wedges. Makes 6 servings.

Per serving: 231 calories, 8 g protein, 32 g carbohydrates, 9 g total fat, 9 mg cholesterol, 78 mg sodium

---

Note: Recipes may be prepared in either a skillet or a wok.

Lime & Chile Monkfish with Corn

Preparation time: About 10 minutes

Cooking time: 10 minutes

Often called "poor man's lobster," monkfish is valued for its delicate flavor and lean, firm flesh.

Monkfish fillets are encased in a tough membrane; you can have the membrane removed at the fish market or do the job yourself, using a sharp knife.

Lime-Chile Sauce (recipe follows)
1½ pounds monkfish fillets
3 tablespoons salad oil
1 cup fresh corn cut from cob or 1 cup frozen whole-kernel corn, thawed and drained
2 tablespoons chopped fresh cilantro (coriander)

Prepare Lime-Chile Sauce; set aside.

Remove and discard membrane from fish. Rinse fish and pat dry, then cut into 1-inch chunks. Place a wok over high heat; when wok is hot, add 2 tablespoons of the oil. When oil is hot, add half the fish; stir-fry until fish flakes when prodded (about 2 minutes). Remove from wok and set aside. Repeat to cook remaining fish, adding remaining 1 tablespoon oil.

Pour Lime-Chile Sauce into wok and bring to a boil, stirring constantly. Add corn and stir until heated through (2 to 3 minutes). Return fish and any accumulated juices to wok; mix gently to heat. Pour onto a warm platter and sprinkle with cilantro. Makes 4 servings.

Lime-Chile Sauce. Stir together ⅓ cup **lime juice;** 3 tablespoons **regular-strength chicken broth;** 1 clove **garlic,** minced or pressed; 1 **small fresh Fresno or jalapeño chile,** minced; ½ teaspoon *each* **ground cumin, pepper,** and **sugar;** and 1 teaspoon **cornstarch.**

Per serving: 268 calories, 26 g protein, 11 g carbohydrates, 13 g total fat, 43 mg cholesterol, 88 mg sodium

Teriyaki Monkfish

Follow directions for **Lime & Chile Monkfish with Corn,** but omit Lime-Chile Sauce. Instead, use this teriyaki sauce: stir together ¼ cup **regular-strength chicken or beef broth,** 2 tablespoons *each* **dry sherry** and **soy sauce,** 2 teaspoons **sugar,** and 1 teaspoon **cornstarch.** Also omit corn; instead, use 1 cup **cooked fresh shelled peas** or 1 cup frozen peas, thawed and drained.

(Pictured on facing page)

Squid & Pea Stir-fry

Preparation time: About 30 minutes

Cooking time: 7 minutes

Its flavor is sweet and delicate—but squid quickly toughens if it's cooked too long. To eliminate the risk of overcooking, start by scoring the squid.

Pan-fried Noodles (recipe follows)
1 pound squid
2 tablespoons salad oil
½ teaspoon minced fresh ginger
1 cup shelled peas (about 1 lb. unshelled)
½ cup regular-strength chicken broth
1 teaspoon soy sauce
1 tablespoon oyster sauce
¼ teaspoon sugar
2 teaspoons cornstarch and 1 tablespoon water, stirred together

Prepare Pan-fried Noodles and keep warm.

To clean each squid, gently pull on body to separate it from hood. Then pull out and discard long, clear quill from hood. Scoop out and discard contents of hood; rinse out hood. Set aside.

With a sharp knife, sever body between eyes and tentacles. Discard eyes and attached material. Pop out and discard hard black beak in center of tentacles. Rinse and drain tentacles; pat dry and set aside.

Pull off and discard thin, speckled membrane from hood; rinse and drain hood. Slit hood lengthwise and open flat. Make ½-inch-wide diagonal cuts across inside of hood. Repeat in opposite direction. Cut scored hood in about 2-inch-square pieces.

Place a wok over medium-high heat; when wok is hot, add 1 tablespoon of the oil. When oil begins to heat, add ginger; stir once. Add squid; stir-fry until edges curl (1½ to 2 minutes). Remove from wok.

Pour remaining 1 tablespoon oil into wok. When oil is hot, add peas and stir-fry for 1 minute. Add broth, soy, oyster sauce, and sugar; bring to a boil and boil for 1 minute. Stir cornstarch-water mixture; pour into wok and stir until sauce boils and thickens. Return squid to wok, stir, and serve at once, over Pan-fried Noodles. Makes 3 or 4 servings.

Pan-fried Noodles. Heat 2 tablespoons **salad oil** in a frying pan over medium-high heat. Spread 8 ounces **Chinese wheat flour noodles,** cooked and drained, in pan in a layer 1 inch thick. Cook until brown on bottom. Turn noodles over in 1 piece; add 1 tablespoon more **salad oil** and cook until browned on other side. Serve whole or in wedges.

Per serving: 473 calories, 27 g protein, 49 g carbohydrates, 19 g total fat, 49 mg cholesterol, 458 mg sodium

---

Note: Recipes may be prepared in either a skillet or a wok.

Because squid toughens if heated too long, Chinese
chefs traditionally score it to hasten cooking. The crosshatching shows in
Squid & Pea Stir-fry (recipe on facing page), here served atop individual
cakes of Pan-fried Noodles.

Squid & Vegetable Stir-fry

Preparation time: About 35 minutes

Cooking time: 10 minutes

Quick stir-frying makes the squid in this savory vegetable mélange as tender as it's tasty. Garlic, ginger, and beef broth give the dish its robust flavor.

        Cooking Sauce (recipe follows)
    1   **pound squid**
    3   **tablespoons salad oil**
    2   **cloves garlic, minced or pressed**
    2   **teaspoons finely minced fresh ginger**
    1   **medium-size onion, thinly sliced**
    ¼   **pound mushrooms, sliced**
    1   **cup sliced celery**
    1   **green bell pepper, seeded and thinly sliced**

Prepare Cooking Sauce and set aside. Clean squid as directed for Squid & Pea Stir-fry (page 54). Slit squid hoods in half lengthwise, then cut crosswise into ¾-inch-wide strips. Leave tentacles whole or cut each into 2 or 3 pieces.

Place a wok over high heat; when wok is hot, add 2 tablespoons of the oil. When oil is hot, add garlic, ginger, and onion and stir-fry for 1 minute. Add mushrooms and stir-fry until mushrooms are soft (about 3 minutes). Remove mixture from wok and set aside.

Pour remaining 1 tablespoon oil into wok. When oil is hot, add squid and stir-fry until edges of hood pieces curl (1½ to 2 minutes). Add celery and bell pepper and stir-fry for 2 more minutes. Return mushroom mixture to wok; stir Cooking Sauce and add. Stir until sauce boils and thickens. Makes 4 servings.

Cooking Sauce. Stir together 1½ tablespoons **cornstarch**, 2 tablespoons **soy sauce**, 1 teaspoon *each* **sugar** and **vinegar**, and ½ cup **regular-strength beef broth.**

Per serving: 213 calories, 17 g protein, 11 g carbohydrates, 11 g total fat, 49 mg cholesterol, 596 mg sodium

Sautéed Oysters with Basil

Preparation time: About 10 minutes

Cooking time: 5 minutes

Made with just five ingredients, this dish could hardly be simpler or quicker. You just brown oysters in butter with a little chopped basil, then make a speedy sauce by stirring white wine into the pan juices.

    ½   **pound shucked fresh oysters, drained**
        All-purpose flour
    2   **tablespoons butter or margarine**
    1   **tablespoon chopped fresh basil or ½ teaspoon dry basil**
    2   **tablespoons dry white wine**

Cut any large oysters into bite-size pieces. Pat oysters dry with paper towels; dredge in flour and shake off excess. Place a wok over medium-high heat; when wok is hot, add butter. When butter is melted, add oysters and sprinkle with basil. Stir-fry until oysters are golden brown (about 3 minutes), then transfer to a serving dish.

Add wine to wok and cook until sauce is reduced to 1 tablespoon. Spoon sauce over oysters. Makes 2 servings.

Per serving: 209 calories, 9 g protein, 11 g carbohydrates, 14 g total fat, 115 mg cholesterol, 201 mg sodium

Gingered Oysters

Preparation time: About 10 minutes

Marinating time: 10 minutes

Cooking time: 5 minutes

Fresh ginger and a sprinkling of Chinese five-spice add a distinctive accent to plump stir-fried oysters. When purchasing fresh ginger, look for firm, unblemished roots with unwrinkled skin; pare off the khaki-colored peel before you slice the root.

    10 **ounces shucked fresh oysters, drained**
    ⅛   **teaspoon Chinese five-spice**
    1½ **teaspoons cornstarch**
    4   **teaspoons soy sauce**
    1½ **tablespoons *each* dry sherry and water**
    10 **green onions (including tops)**
    2   **tablespoons salad oil**
    4   **thin, dime-size slices fresh ginger**

Cut any large oysters into bite-size pieces. In a bowl, stir together five-spice and 1 teaspoon *each* of the cornstarch and soy. Add oysters and stir to coat; let marinate for 10 minutes. Meanwhile, in another bowl, blend remaining ½ teaspoon cornstarch, remaining 1 tablespoon soy, sherry, and water; set aside. Also cut onions in half lengthwise, then cut crosswise into 1½-inch lengths.

Place a wok over medium-high heat; when wok is hot, add 1 tablespoon of the oil. When oil begins to heat, add ginger and stir-fry for 10 seconds; then add onions and stir-fry for 30 seconds. Remove ginger and onions from wok.

Reduce heat to medium. Pour remaining 1 tablespoon oil into wok. When oil is hot, add oysters and stir-fry until slightly firm (about 2 minutes). Return ginger and onions to wok. Stir cornstarch-sherry mixture; pour into wok and stir until sauce boils and thickens. Remove ginger, if desired. Makes 2 or 3 servings.

Per serving: 172 calories, 8 g protein, 9 g carbohydrates, 11 g total fat, 71 mg cholesterol, 530 mg sodium

Lobster Cantonese

Preparation time: About 15 minutes

Cooking time: 10 minutes

If you see "lobster sauce" on the menu in a Chinese restaurant, chances are it's something like the cooking sauce used in this dish. Though it doesn't contain lobster (it's just a mixture of broth, soy, sherry, and a little cornstarch and white pepper), it's traditionally used with lobster. The same sauce enhances other shellfish, too; try it with crab, scallops, or shrimp.

Cooking Sauce (recipe follows)
- 1½ **pounds raw lobster tails (thawed if frozen)**
- 3 **tablespoons salad oil**
- 2 **tablespoons fermented salted black beans, rinsed, drained, and finely chopped**
- 2 **cloves garlic, finely chopped**
- 1 **teaspoon minced fresh ginger**
- ¼ **pound lean boneless pork (such as shoulder or butt), trimmed of excess fat and finely chopped or ground**
- 1 **green onion (including top), thinly sliced**
- 1 **egg, lightly beaten**

Prepare Cooking Sauce and set aside. If you want to cook lobster in the shell, trim side fins; then cut tails in half lengthwise and devein. Cut large pieces in half crosswise. If you prefer to cook lobster out of the shell, remove meat from shell and cut into bite-size pieces.

Place a wok over high heat; when wok is hot, add oil. When oil begins to heat, add black beans, garlic, and ginger; stir once. Then add pork and stir-fry until no longer pink (about 2 minutes).

Add lobster and stir-fry until shells turn red or until shelled meat is opaque throughout; cut to test (3 to 4 minutes). Stir Cooking Sauce, add to wok, and stir until sauce boils and thickens. Add onion and egg; stir just until egg begins to set (about 30 seconds). Makes 3 or 4 servings.

Cooking Sauce. Stir together 1 tablespoon *each* **cornstarch, soy sauce,** and **dry sherry;** ½ cup **regular-strength chicken broth;** and a dash of **white pepper.**

Per serving: 297 calories, 29 g protein, 5 g carbohydrates, 17 g total fat, 184 mg cholesterol, 901 mg sodium

Crab Cantonese

Follow directions for **Lobster Cantonese,** but use 1 large **cooked crab in shell** (1½ to 2 lbs.), cleaned and cracked, in place of lobster. Cut body into quarters; leave legs and claws whole. Cook crab until heated through (3 to 4 minutes).

Shrimp Cantonese

Follow directions for **Lobster Cantonese,** but use 1 pound **medium-size raw shrimp** in place of lobster. Cut through backs of shells with scissors and devein, or remove shells and devein. Cook shrimp until they turn pink (about 3 minutes).

Scallops Cantonese

Follow directions for **Lobster Cantonese,** but use 1 pound **scallops** (thawed if frozen) in place of lobster. Rinse scallops and pat dry, then cut into ¼-inch-thick slices. Cook scallops just until opaque throughout; cut to test (about 3 minutes).

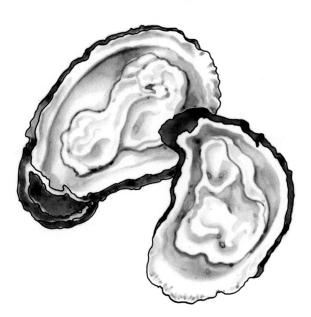

Note: Recipes may be prepared in either a skillet or a wok.

Use fingers—not forks or chopsticks—to enjoy Crab Curry
(recipe on facing page). Once you get started, it's hard to stop until
the last bite of this Cantonese specialty has disappeared! Pass around a
basket of hot, damp cloths after the meal.

Crab in Black Bean Sauce

Preparation time: About 15 minutes

Cooking time: 5 minutes

If you cook crab in its shell, the meat stays especially succulent—and the preparation time stays brief. Like our Crab Curry (at right), this is finger food; it's a good choice for an informal meal.

- 1 **large cooked crab in shell (1½ to 2 lbs.), cleaned and cracked**
- 2 **tablespoons salad oil**
- 1½ **tablespoons fermented salted black beans, rinsed, drained, and finely chopped**
- 1 **large clove garlic, minced or pressed**
- ¾ **teaspoon minced fresh ginger**
- 1 **green bell pepper, seeded and cut into 1-inch squares**
- 1 **tablespoon *each* soy sauce and dry sherry**
- 2 **green onions (including tops), cut into 1-inch lengths**
- ⅓ **cup regular-strength chicken broth**

Cut crab body into quarters; leave legs and claws whole. Set aside.

Place a wok over high heat; when wok is hot, add oil. When oil begins to heat, add black beans, garlic, and ginger and stir once. Add bell pepper and stir-fry for 1 minute. Add crab, soy, sherry, onions, and broth; stir until crab is heated through (about 3 minutes). Makes 2 servings.

Per serving: 328 calories, 22 g protein, 7 g carbohydrates, 24 g total fat, 114 mg cholesterol, 1,248 mg sodium

Crab in Tomato-Garlic Sauce

Follow directions for **Crab in Black Bean Sauce,** but increase garlic to 3 cloves and omit black beans and ginger. Add 2 large **tomatoes,** peeled, seeded, and chopped, along with bell pepper. Omit soy, sherry, and broth; instead, use ½ cup **dry white wine.**

Crab in Cream Sauce

Follow directions for **Crab in Black Bean Sauce,** using 1 tablespoon minced **shallots** and 1 **red bell pepper,** seeded and cut into 1-inch squares, in place of the black beans, ginger, and green bell pepper. Substitute ¼ cup **whipping cream,** 2 tablespoon **dry white wine,** 1 teaspoon **Dijon mustard,** and 1 tablespoon chopped **parsley** for the soy, sherry, green onions, and broth.

(Pictured on facing page)

Crab Curry

Preparation time: About 15 minutes

Cooking time: 10 minutes

This mild Cantonese curry of crab and vegetables is appealing to the eye and fun to eat, too. Finger food can be messy, though, so pass a basket of damp cloths around the table at the end of the meal.

- **Cooking Sauce (recipe follows)**
- 1 **teaspoon *each* salt and sugar**
- 4 **teaspoons curry powder**
- ¼ **pound lean boneless pork (such as shoulder or butt), trimmed of excess fat and finely chopped or ground**
- 1 **large cooked crab in shell (1½ to 2 lbs.), cleaned and cracked**
- 3 **tablespoons salad oil**
- 1 **large clove garlic, minced**
- 1 **medium-size onion, cut into wedges, layers separated**
- 1 **medium-size green bell pepper, seeded and cut into 1-inch squares**
- 1 **egg, lightly beaten**

Prepare Cooking Sauce and set aside. Sprinkle salt, sugar, and curry powder over pork; mix well and set aside. Cut crab body into quarters; leave legs and claws whole. Set crab aside.

Place a wok over high heat. When wok is hot, add oil. When oil begins to heat, add garlic and stir once; then add seasoned pork and stir-fry until no longer pink (about 2 minutes). Add onion and bell pepper and stir-fry for 1 minute. Add crab and stir often until heated through (about 3 minutes). Stir Cooking Sauce, pour into wok, and stir until sauce boils and thickens. Add egg; stir just until egg begins to set (about 30 seconds). Makes 3 or 4 servings.

Cooking Sauce. Stir together ¾ cup **regular-strength chicken broth** and 1 tablespoon *each* **cornstarch, soy sauce,** and **dry sherry.**

Per serving: 252 calories, 18 g protein, 8 g carbohydrates, 16 g total fat, 145 mg cholesterol, 1,155 mg sodium

Shrimp Curry

Follow directions for **Crab Curry,** but use 1 pound **medium-size raw shrimp,** shelled and deveined, in place of crab. Stir-fry shrimp until they turn pink (about 3 minutes).

Note: Recipes may be prepared in either a skillet or a wok.

Hot & Sour Shrimp

Preparation time: About 20 minutes

Cooking time: About 10 minutes

The pungent power of garlic and ginger comes through in this piquant shrimp and vegetable dish. Though it's a Szechwan recipe, it's not overwhelmingly spicy; if you want it hotter, increase the quantity of crushed red pepper.

- 1 **pound medium-size raw shrimp, shelled and deveined**
- 1 **tablespoon dry sherry**
  Cooking Sauce (recipe follows)
- 3 **tablespoons salad oil**
- 3 **cloves garlic, minced or pressed**
- 1½ **tablespoons minced fresh ginger**
- ¼ **teaspoon crushed red pepper**
- 2 **large stalks celery, cut into ½-inch-thick slices**
- ½ **cup sliced bamboo shoots**
- 2 **green onions (including tops), thinly sliced**

In a bowl, toss shrimp with sherry. Prepare Cooking Sauce and set aside.

Place a wok over high heat; when wok is hot, add 1½ tablespoons of the oil. When oil begins to heat, add garlic, ginger, and red pepper; stir once. Then add shrimp and stir-fry until shrimp turn pink (about 3 minutes). Remove from wok and set aside.

Pour remaining 1½ tablespoons oil into wok. When oil is hot, add celery and bamboo shoots and stir-fry for 1 minute. Stir Cooking Sauce, then pour into wok. Stir in shrimp and onions. Stir until sauce boils and thickens. Makes 3 or 4 servings.

Cooking Sauce. Stir together ¼ cup **distilled white vinegar,** 2 tablespoons **soy sauce,** 5 teaspoons **sugar,** and 2 teaspoons **cornstarch.**

Per serving: 236 calories, 21 g protein, 12 g carbohydrates, 12 g total fat, 131 mg cholesterol, 731 mg sodium

Shrimp & Cucumber Stir-fry

Preparation time: About 15 minutes

Cooking time: About 10 minutes

A winning combination of textures and tastes—crunchy cucumbers, succulent shrimp, and lively seasonings—makes this dish a standout.

- **Cooking Sauce (recipe follows)**
- 2 **large cucumbers, peeled**
- 3 **tablespoons salad oil**
- 2 **tablespoons minced fresh ginger**
- 1 **clove garlic, minced or pressed**
- ¼ **cup minced green onions (including tops)**
- 1 **pound medium-size raw shrimp, shelled and deveined**
  Salt

Prepare Cooking Sauce and set aside.

Cut cucumbers in half lengthwise; scrape out and discard seeds. Cut each cucumber half crosswise into ¼-inch-thick slices.

Place a wok over high heat; when wok is hot, add 1 tablespoon of the oil. When oil is hot, add cucumbers and 1 tablespoon of the ginger; stir-fry until cucumbers are tender-crisp to bite (about 3 minutes). Pour onto a platter and keep warm.

Pour remaining 2 tablespoons oil into wok; when oil is hot, add garlic, remaining 1 tablespoon ginger, onions, and shrimp. Stir-fry until shrimp turn pink (about 3 minutes). Stir Cooking Sauce, pour into wok, and stir until sauce boils and thickens. Season to taste with salt, then pour over cucumbers. Makes 3 or 4 servings.

Cooking Sauce. Stir together 3 tablespoons **dry sherry** or regular-strength chicken broth, 2 tablespoons **distilled white vinegar,** 1½ tablespoons **soy sauce,** 1 teaspoon **cornstarch,** and ½ teaspoon **sugar.**

Per serving: 224 calories, 21 g protein, 9 g carbohydrates, 12 g total fat, 131 mg cholesterol, 588 mg sodium

Shrimp Flambé

Preparation time: About 20 minutes

Cooking time: About 10 minutes

The assertive flavors of curry, paprika, garlic, and brandy blend beautifully in a rich-tasting sauce for shrimp. If you have an electric wok, you can flame the entrée right at the table.

- 2 tablespoons butter or margarine
- 2 cloves garlic, minced or pressed
- 1½ teaspoons curry powder
- ½ teaspoon paprika
- ⅓ cup thinly sliced green onions (including tops)
- 2 tablespoons finely chopped fresh cilantro (coriander)
- 1 pound medium-size raw shrimp, shelled, deveined, and butterflied
- 2 tablespoons *each* purchased teriyaki sauce and water
- 2 tablespoons brandy
- 3 or 4 slices French bread, toasted and buttered

Place a wok over medium heat; when wok is hot, add butter. When butter is melted, add garlic and curry powder; stir for 1 minute. Stir in paprika, onions, cilantro, and shrimp. Stir-fry until shrimp turn pink (about 3 minutes). Stir in teriyaki sauce and water and heat through. Also pour brandy into a small pan and warm over low heat until bubbly.

Carefully pour warm brandy over surface of shrimp mixture and ignite (not beneath an exhaust fan or near flammable items). When flames die down, spoon shrimp and juices evenly over toast. Makes 3 or 4 servings.

Per serving: 291 calories, 23 g protein, 23 g carbohydrates, 11 g total fat, 155 mg cholesterol, 829 mg sodium

Sautéed Shrimp in Mint Beurre Blanc

Preparation time: About 15 minutes

Cooking time: 10 minutes

Rich yet refreshing—that describes this dish. Juicy pink shrimp are cloaked in a minted wine and butter sauce that's lightly accented with lemon peel.

- 6 to 8 tablespoons butter or margarine
- ½ teaspoon grated lemon peel
- 1 cup lightly packed fresh mint leaves
- 1 pound medium-size raw shrimp, shelled and deveined
- 1 cup dry white wine
  Lemon slices and fresh mint sprigs

In a food processor or blender, whirl 4 tablespoons of the butter, lemon peel, and mint leaves until well blended; scoop into a cup. If made ahead, cover and refrigerate until next day.

Place a wok over medium heat; when wok is hot, add 2 tablespoons of the remaining plain butter.

When butter is melted, add shrimp and stir-fry until shrimp turn pink (about 3 minutes). With a slotted spoon, lift out shrimp; keep warm.

Increase heat to high. Pour wine into wok, bring to a boil, and boil, stirring, until wine is reduced to ⅓ cup (about 5 minutes). Add mint butter all at once; stir quickly until melted and blended into sauce. For a thicker sauce, stir in 2 tablespoons more plain butter. Arrange shrimp in wok, or pour sauce into a serving dish and top with shrimp. Garnish with lemon slices and mint sprigs. Makes 4 servings.

Per serving: 304 calories, 20 g protein, 1 g carbohydrate, 24 g total fat, 193 mg cholesterol, 429 mg sodium

Shrimp with Asparagus & Tomatillos

Preparation time: About 20 minutes

Cooking time: About 10 minutes

Shrimp and asparagus take on a bit of Mexican flavor when you add diced tomatillos and fresh cilantro to the sauce. Tomatillos look and taste something like green tomatoes; they're sold in Mexican markets, specialty produce stores, and many well-stocked supermarkets.

- 1 pound asparagus
- 3 tablespoons butter or margarine
- 3 tablespoons olive oil or salad oil
- 1 cup diced celery
- 2 tomatillos *each* about 2 inches in diameter, husked, cored, and diced
- ½ cup chopped fresh cilantro (coriander)
- 1 tablespoon chopped fresh mint
- 1½ tablespoons lemon juice
- 1 pound medium-size raw shrimp, shelled and deveined
  Salt and pepper

Snap off and discard tough ends of asparagus, then cut spears into ½-inch slanting slices. Set aside.

Place a wok over high heat; when wok is hot, add butter and oil. When butter is melted, add asparagus, celery, tomatillos, and cilantro. Stir-fry for 2 minutes. Add mint, lemon juice, and shrimp; stir-fry until shrimp turn pink and asparagus is tender-crisp to bite (3 to 5 more minutes). Season to taste with salt and pepper. Makes 4 servings.

Per serving: 291 calories, 22 g protein, 6 g carbohydrates, 21 g total fat, 154 mg cholesterol, 309 mg sodium

Note: Recipes may be prepared in either a skillet or a wok.

Shrimp Pesto Stir-fry

Preparation time: 15 minutes

Cooking time: 12 minutes

Shrimp teams well with a pesto sauce redolent of basil. Make the pesto from fresh basil if you can find it, or use our quick version made with dried herbs.

  Quick Pesto Sauce (recipe follows) or 2 tablespoons Fresh Pesto (page 84)
3 **tablespoons butter or margarine**
1 **carrot, cut into ¼-inch-thick slices**
1 **small onion, cut into 1-inch-square pieces**
1 **small zucchini, cut into ¼-inch-thick slices**
8 **to 10 small mushrooms, sliced**
½ **small green bell pepper, seeded and sliced lengthwise**
½ **small red bell pepper, seeded and sliced lengthwise**
¾ **pound medium-size raw shrimp, shelled and deveined**
  Fresh basil sprigs (optional)
  Grated Parmesan cheese (optional)
  Hot cooked rice (optional)

Prepare Quick Pesto Sauce; set aside.

Place a wok over medium-high heat; when wok is hot, add 1 tablespoon of the butter. When butter is melted, add carrot and onion and stir-fry for 2 minutes. Add 1 tablespoon more butter, zucchini, mushrooms, and green and red bell pepper; stir-fry just until carrot is tender-crisp to bite (about 2 more minutes). Remove vegetables from wok and keep warm.

Add remaining 1 tablespoon butter to wok; when butter is melted, stir in Quick Pesto Sauce. Add shrimp and stir-fry until they turn pink (3 to 4 minutes). Return vegetables to wok and stir until vegetables are hot and coated with sauce.

Turn shrimp-vegetable mixture into a shallow serving dish; garnish with basil and sprinkle with cheese, if desired. Serve with rice, if desired. Makes 2 servings.

Quick Pesto Sauce. Stir together 1 tablespoon grated **Parmesan cheese,** 2 teaspoons *each* **dry basil** and **parsley flakes,** and 1 tablespoon **olive oil** or salad oil.

Per serving: 415 calories, 31 g protein, 11 g carbohydrates, 28 g total fat, 259 mg cholesterol, 444 mg sodium

Scallop Pesto Stir-fry

Follow directions for **Shrimp Pesto Stir-fry,** but in place of shrimp, use ½ to ¾ pound **scallops** (thawed if frozen). Rinse scallops and pat dry, then cut into ¼-inch-thick slices. Cook scallops until opaque throughout; cut to test (3 to 4 minutes).

(Pictured on facing page)

Snow Peas with Shrimp

Preparation time: About 20 minutes

Cooking time: 5 minutes

For a meal in minutes, try this snappy stir-fry of shrimp, water chestnuts, and sweet snow peas. If you like, leave the tails on the shrimp for an attractive presentation.

  Cooking Sauce (recipe follows)
3 **tablespoons salad oil**
1 **clove garlic, minced or pressed**
1 **pound medium-size raw shrimp, shelled and deveined**
1½ **cups Chinese pea pods (also called snow or sugar peas) or sugar snap peas, ends and strings removed; or 1 package (6 oz.) frozen Chinese pea pods, thawed and drained**
1 **can (about 8 oz.) water chestnuts, drained and thinly sliced**
2 **or 3 green onions (including tops), thinly sliced**

Prepare Cooking Sauce and set aside.

Place a wok over high heat; when wok is hot, add oil. When oil is hot, add garlic and shrimp and stir-fry for about 1 minute. Add pea pods and stir-fry for about 3 minutes (30 seconds if using frozen pea pods). Add water chestnuts and onions; stir to mix. Stir Cooking Sauce and add; stir until sauce boils and thickens and shrimp turn pink. Makes 4 servings.

Cooking Sauce. Stir together 1 teaspoon **cornstarch** and ¼ teaspoon **ground ginger.** Stir in 2 tablespoons *each* **soy sauce** and **dry sherry** and ½ cup **regular-strength chicken broth.**

Per serving: 244 calories, 22 g protein, 11 g carbohydrates, 12 g total fat, 131 mg cholesterol, 850 mg sodium

Note: Recipes may be prepared in either a skillet or a wok.

Pink shrimp and crunchy water chestnuts share the wok with
bright green snow peas in this quick, colorful stir-fry. When shelling
shrimp for Snow Peas with Shrimp (recipe on facing page), leave the
tails in place for a decorative look.

Bahia Shrimp Sauté

Preparation time: 25 minutes

Cooking time: 20 minutes

A pungent blend of spices permeates an exotic Brazilian stir-fry of succulent pink shrimp and lightly cooked vegetables. Garnish each serving with peanuts and toasted coconut.

> About ¾ pound spinach
> ¼ cup unsweetened flaked coconut
> 3 tablespoons salad oil
> 1 pound medium-size raw shrimp, shelled and deveined
> 1 medium-size onion, chopped
> 1 clove garlic, minced or pressed
> ½ pound green beans (ends removed), cut into 1-inch pieces
> ¼ teaspoon *each* ground ginger, ground cumin, ground coriander, crushed red pepper, and paprika
> ¼ cup water
> Salt and black pepper
> ¼ cup dry-roasted peanuts

Discard spinach stems and any tough or wilted leaves. Rinse remaining leaves well, pat dry, and cut into short shreds. Set aside. Place a wok over medium heat; when wok is hot, add coconut and stir until golden. Pour out and set aside.

Increase heat to high. Pour 2 tablespoons of the oil into wok; when oil is hot, add shrimp. Stir-fry until shrimp turn pink (about 3 minutes). With a slotted spoon, lift out shrimp; set aside. Pour remaining 1 tablespoon oil into wok; when oil is hot, add onion and garlic and stir-fry until onion is soft.

Stir in beans, ginger, cumin, coriander, red pepper, and paprika. Stir-fry for 1 minute; then add water, cover, and cook, stirring often, until beans are tender-crisp to bite (about 4 more minutes). Add spinach and stir for 1 minute; then return shrimp to wok and cook just until heated through (about 1 more minute). Season to taste with salt and black pepper; sprinkle with coconut and peanuts. Makes 4 servings.

Per serving: 306 calories, 25 g protein, 12 g carbohydrates, 19 g total fat, 131 mg cholesterol, 324 mg sodium

Scallops & Shrimp in Béarnaise Cream

Preparation time: 15 minutes

Cooking time: 20 minutes

The sauce isn't true béarnaise, but the traditional ingredients are here: reduced vinegar, shallots, tarragon. You might accompany this elegant entrée with steamed broccoli, green beans, or another fresh green vegetable of your choice.

> 1 pound scallops (thawed if frozen)
> 2 tablespoons butter or margarine
> ½ pound large raw shrimp, shelled, deveined, and split lengthwise
> ⅓ cup minced shallots
> ¾ cup tarragon wine vinegar or white wine vinegar
> ½ cup regular-strength chicken broth
> ¼ teaspoon dry tarragon
> 1 tablespoon Dijon mustard
> ½ cup whipping cream
> Salt and white pepper

Rinse scallops and pat dry; cut any large scallops in half.

Place a wok over medium-high heat; when wok is hot, add butter. When butter is melted, add scallops and shrimp. Stir-fry just until shrimp turn pink and scallops are opaque throughout; cut to test (3 to 5 minutes). Lift out scallops and shrimp and keep warm.

Increase heat to high. Add shallots, vinegar, broth, and tarragon to wok. Bring to a boil; boil until reduced to ½ cup. Pour any accumulated juices from scallops and shrimp into wok along with mustard and cream. Boil until sauce is reduced to about ¾ cup. Add scallops and shrimp; stir until heated through. Season to taste with salt and white pepper. Makes 4 servings.

Per serving: 314 calories, 31 g protein, 9 g carbohydrates, 17 g total fat, 155 mg cholesterol, 586 mg sodium

Scallop & Shrimp Curry

Preparation time: 20 minutes

Cooking time: 20 minutes

Delightfully rich and spicy is this creamy curry of shrimp and scallops. If you use an imported curry powder from a spice shop (or mix up your own blend), you may want to adjust the amount used; imported powders are often hotter than domestic brands.

¾ **pound scallops (thawed if frozen)**
¼ **cup butter or margarine**
1 **small onion, finely chopped**
2 **cloves garlic, minced or pressed**
2 **to 3 teaspoons curry powder**
1 **pound medium-size raw shrimp, shelled and deveined**
1 **cup whipping cream**
½ **cup dry white wine**
½ **teaspoon dry summer savory leaves**
2 **tablespoons water**
1 **tablespoon cornstarch**
 Salt and pepper
 Hot cooked rice

Rinse scallops and pat dry; cut any large scallops in half. Set aside.

Place a wok over medium heat; when wok is hot, add 2 tablespoons of the butter. When butter is melted, add onion, garlic, and curry powder and stir-fry until onion is soft. Add remaining 2 tablespoons butter; when butter is melted, add scallops and shrimp. Stir-fry just until shrimp turn pink and scallops are opaque throughout; cut to test (3 to 5 minutes). With a slotted spoon, lift out scallops and shrimp; keep warm.

Add cream, wine, and summer savory to wok; blend water with cornstarch and stir into cream mixture. Cook, stirring, until sauce boils and thickens. Return scallops and shrimp to wok; stir until heated through. Season to taste with salt and pepper; serve over rice. Makes 4 to 6 servings.

Per serving: 312 calories, 24 g protein, 5 g carbohydrates, 22 g total fat, 172 mg cholesterol, 313 mg sodium

Scallops in Garlic Butter

Preparation time: About 10 minutes

Cooking time: About 10 minutes

Toasted almonds add a little crunch to a super-simple stir-fry of scallops seasoned with lemon peel and plenty of garlic.

1 **to 1½ pounds scallops (thawed if frozen)**
3 **tablespoons sliced almonds**
¼ **cup butter**
5 **large cloves garlic, minced or pressed**
2 **tablespoons chopped parsley**
1 **teaspoon grated lemon peel**

Rinse scallops and pat dry; then cut any large scallops in half. Set aside.

Place a wok over medium heat; when wok is hot, add almonds and stir until golden (about 2 minutes). Pour out of wok and set aside.

Add butter; when butter is melted, add garlic, parsley, and lemon peel and stir for about 1 minute. Add scallops (a portion at a time, if necessary) and stir-fry just until opaque throughout; cut to test (3 to 4 minutes). Transfer scallop mixture to a platter, top with almonds, and serve immediately. Makes 4 servings.

Per serving: 290 calories, 31 g protein, 6 g carbohydrates, 15 g total fat, 94 mg cholesterol, 393 mg sodium

Tarragon Scallop Sauté

Preparation time: About 10 minutes

Cooking time: About 10 minutes

If you like your scallops flavored with tarragon, try this easy stir-fry: just scallops, mushrooms, and shallots, seasoned with the dry herb and finished at the table with a squeeze of lemon.

1 **pound scallops (thawed if frozen)**
6 **tablespoons butter or margarine**
½ **teaspoon dry tarragon**
3 **tablespoons chopped shallots or green onions (white part only)**
½ **pound mushrooms, sliced**
2 **tablespoons dry white wine**
 Chopped parsley
 Lemon wedges

Rinse scallops, pat dry, and cut into bite-size pieces. Set aside.

Place a wok over medium-high heat; when wok is hot, add butter. When butter is melted, add tarragon, shallots, and mushrooms; stir-fry until mushrooms are soft. Push mushrooms to side of wok and add scallops. Stir-fry until scallops are opaque throughout; cut to test (3 to 4 minutes). Sprinkle wine over scallops and cook for 1 more minute; then stir together scallops and mushrooms. Garnish each serving with parsley and lemon wedges. Makes 3 or 4 servings.

Per serving: 276 calories, 21 g protein, 7 g carbohydrates, 18 g total fat, 88 mg cholesterol, 362 mg sodium

Note: Recipes may be prepared in either a skillet or a wok.

In China, fried rice in countless variations is a standard vehicle
for leftovers. Try Fried Rice with Ham & Peanuts (recipe on facing page)
and you'll understand its popularity, whether you
use leftovers or not.

Noodles & Rice

(Pictured on facing page)

Fried Rice with Ham & Peanuts

Preparation time: About 10 minutes

Cooking time: About 10 minutes

Fried rice is a classic quick meal, easily embellished with leftover meat and your favorite vegetables. For best success, start with *cold* cooked rice; if it's warm or hot, the grains will stick together.

- 2 cups cold cooked long-grain white rice
- 2 eggs
- ¼ teaspoon salt
- ¼ cup salad oil
- 1 small onion, chopped
- 1 clove garlic, minced or pressed
- 1 medium-size green bell pepper, seeded and diced
- ¼ pound mushrooms, chopped
- ½ pound cold cooked ham, chicken, turkey, or pork, diced (about 1½ cups)
- ½ cup salted roasted peanuts
- 2 tablespoons soy sauce
  Tomato wedges and cucumber slices

Rub cooked rice with wet hands so all grains are separated; set aside. In a small bowl, lightly beat together eggs and salt.

Place a wok over medium heat; when wok is hot, add 1 tablespoon of the oil. When oil is hot, add eggs and cook, stirring occasionally, until soft curds form; remove from wok and set aside.

Increase heat to medium-high; add 1 tablespoon more oil to wok. When oil is hot, add onion and garlic. Stir-fry until onion is soft; then add bell pepper, mushrooms, ham, and peanuts. Stir-fry until heated through (about 2 minutes). Remove from wok and set aside.

Pour remaining 2 tablespoons oil into wok. When oil is hot, add rice and stir-fry until heated through (about 2 minutes); stir in ham mixture and soy. Add eggs; stir mixture gently until eggs are in small pieces. Garnish with tomato and cucumber. Makes 4 servings.

Per serving: 467 calories, 24 g protein, 25 g carbohydrates, 31 g total fat, 170 mg cholesterol, 1,616 mg sodium

Cajun Dirty Rice

Preparation time: About 10 minutes

Cooking time: About 15 minutes

This rice may be "dirty," but it's delicious! It's one of the most popular dishes in Louisiana. Vary the spiciness by adding cayenne to taste; real Cajuns like it fiery.

- ¼ pound chicken giblets, including liver
- ¼ cup salad oil
- ½ pound lean ground beef
- 2 stalks celery, chopped
- 1 red bell pepper, seeded and chopped
- 1 medium-size onion, chopped
- 2 teaspoons all-purpose flour
- ½ to 2 teaspoons ground red pepper (cayenne)
- 2 teaspoons paprika
- 1½ teaspoons dry oregano leaves
- 1 cup regular-strength chicken broth
- 3 cups cold cooked white rice
- 2 green onions (including tops), thinly sliced
  Salt and black pepper

Using a sharp knife, trim giblets of any hard membranes or connective tissue. Finely chop giblets or grind them in a food processor.

Place a wok over high heat; when wok is hot, add 2 tablespoons of the oil. When oil is hot, add giblets and beef and cook, stirring, until no longer pink (about 4 minutes). Using a slotted spoon, transfer to a small bowl and set aside.

Pour remaining 2 tablespoons oil into wok; when oil is hot, add celery, bell pepper, and chopped onion. Stir-fry until vegetables are soft (about 7 minutes). Sprinkle in flour, red pepper, paprika, and oregano; cook until flour is browned (about 1 minute). Pour in broth, bring to a boil, and stir in giblets and beef. Add rice and stir-fry until heated through (about 3 minutes); stir in green onions. Season to taste with salt and black pepper. Makes 6 servings.

Per serving: 315 calories, 13 g protein, 23 g carbohydrates, 19 g total fat, 78 mg cholesterol, 221 mg sodium

Vegetarian Dirty Rice

Follow directions for **Cajun Dirty Rice,** using ½ cup **peanuts** in place of the giblets and ground beef, and stir-frying until golden (about 2 minutes). Replace broth with 1 cup **water** and white rice with 3 cups cold cooked **brown rice.**

Note: Recipes may be prepared in either a skillet or a wok.

Rice & Bean Sprouts

Preparation time: 5 minutes

Cooking time: About 35 minutes

Stickier in texture than the familiar long-grain white rice, short-grain rice is favored by Korean, Japanese, and Filipino cooks. Here, hot steamed rice is combined with crunchy bean sprouts and characteristic Korean seasonings of soy and sesame for a filling side dish.

   2   cups hot Steamed Short-grain Rice (recipe follows)
   3   tablespoons sesame seeds
   1   tablespoon salad oil
   2   green onions (including tops), minced
   1   clove garlic, minced or pressed
 1½   cups bean sprouts
   2   tablespoons soy sauce

Prepare steamed rice. Meanwhile, place a wok over medium heat; when wok is hot, add sesame seeds and stir until golden (about 2 minutes). Pour seeds out of wok; crush coarsely with a mortar and pestle or whirl very briefly in a blender. Set aside.

Measure out 2 cups of the cooked rice; keep warm. (Reserve remaining rice for other uses.)

Return wok to medium heat; when wok is hot, add oil. When oil is hot, add sesame seeds, onions, and garlic; stir-fry until onions are soft. Add bean sprouts and stir until heated through.

Add rice and soy to wok; mix gently, being careful not to mash rice grains. Makes about 4 servings.

Steamed Short-grain Rice. Place 1 cup **short-grain rice** (such as pearl) in a heavy 1½- to 2-quart pan. Cover with **cold water,** stir, and drain; repeat until water is clear. To drained rice, add 1¼ cups **cold water** and, if desired, ½ teaspoon **salt.** Bring to a boil over high heat. Reduce heat to low, cover, and simmer for 20 minutes without lifting lid. Remove from heat and let stand, covered, for 5 to 10 minutes. Uncover; fluff with a fork. Makes about 3½ cups.

Per serving: 297 calories, 7 g protein, 51 g carbohydrates, 7 g total fat, 0 mg cholesterol, 834 mg sodium

Tomato Fried Rice

Preparation time: About 5 minutes

Cooking time: About 10 minutes

Colors remain bright in this quick rice dish. To vary the flavor of the rice, omit the salt and add about a tablespoon of soy sauce with the sherry.

   2   tablespoons salad oil
   2   tablespoons butter or margarine
   1   small onion, finely chopped
   3   cups cold cooked rice
  ½   teaspoon *each* salt and sugar
       Dash of pepper
   1   jar (2 oz.) sliced pimentos, drained
       About 2 tablespoons dry sherry, white wine, or water
   2   medium-size tomatoes, peeled, seeded, and diced
       Chopped parsley or sliced green onion tops

Place a wok over medium-high heat; when wok is hot, add oil and butter. When butter is melted, add onion and stir-fry until tender-crisp to bite (about 2 minutes).

Add rice and stir-fry until rice is golden (about 7 minutes). Stir in salt, sugar, pepper, pimentos, and 2 tablespoons of the sherry. Continue to stir, adding a little more sherry if needed, for about 1 more minute. Stir in tomatoes and cook for 1 to 2 more minutes.

Spoon into a serving dish and sprinkle with parsley. Makes 4 to 6 servings.

Per serving: 169 calories, 2 g protein, 21 g carbohydrates, 9 g total fat, 10 mg cholesterol, 227 mg sodium

Soft-fried Noodles

Preparation time: About 10 minutes

Cooking time: About 15 minutes

A sweet-hot sauce melds all the flavors in this Thai dish of rice noodles, pork, shrimp, and vegetables. You may see rice noodles sold as *mai fun;* they're available in many well-stocked supermarkets.

       Sweet-Hot Sauce (recipe follows)
       Soy-Pepper Sauce (recipe follows)
   6   ounces dried thin rice noodles (rice sticks)
       About 3 quarts boiling salted water
   5   tablespoons salad oil
  ¼   pound medium-size raw shrimp, shelled, deveined, and chopped
   1   medium-size onion, chopped
  ½   pound lean ground pork
   2   cloves garlic, minced or pressed
   1   medium-size carrot, shredded
   2   eggs, lightly beaten
  ¼   cup finely chopped roasted peanuts
       Garnishes: ⅓ pound bean sprouts, coarsely chopped; 3 green onions (including tops), cut into thin strips; and 1 lime, cut into wedges

Prepare Sweet-Hot Sauce and Soy-Pepper Sauce; set both aside. Cook noodles in about 3 quarts boiling salted water until barely tender to bite (2 to 4 minutes). Drain, rinse with cold water, and drain again.

Place a wok over high heat. When wok is hot, add 1 tablespoon of the oil; when oil is hot, add shrimp and stir-fry until pink (1 to 2 minutes). Remove from wok and set aside.

Pour 1 tablespoon more oil into wok; when oil is hot, add onion and crumble in pork. Stir-fry until pork is lightly browned (abut 4 minutes). Add garlic and carrot and stir-fry for 1 more minute. Add 2 tablespoons more oil; add drained noodles and stir until heated through.

Make a well in center of noodle mixture and pour in remaining 1 tablespoon oil. Pour eggs into well. Cook, stirring (keep eggs in well), just until eggs begin to set; then stir eggs into noodle mixture. Return shrimp to wok and add Sweet-Hot Sauce; stir to blend. Pour into a serving dish and sprinkle with peanuts. Surround with garnishes and serve with Soy-Pepper Sauce. Makes 3 or 4 servings.

Sweet-Hot Sauce. Stir together 2 teaspoons *each* **distilled white vinegar** and **water,** ½ teaspoon **crushed red pepper,** 2 tablespoons **fish sauce** (*nam pla*) or soy sauce, and 1 tablespoon *each* minced **fresh cilantro** (coriander) and **sugar.**

Soy-Pepper Sauce. Stir together 6 tablespoons **soy sauce** and ½ to ¾ teaspoon **crushed red pepper.**

Per serving: 566 calories, 27 g protein, 47 g carbohydrates, 30 g total fat, 208 mg cholesterol, 2,232 mg sodium

Noodles & Beef with Black Bean Sauce

Preparation time: About 10 minutes

Marinating time: 15 minutes

Cooking time: 25 minutes

Pungent fermented black beans, thin strips of beef, and egg noodles make a hearty dish with a decidedly Oriental accent. Black beans are widely available in supermarkets; you'll find them in jars or small plastic bags.

- 4 ounces dried medium-wide noodles
  Boiling salted water
- ¼ cup salad oil
- ½ pond lean boneless beef steak (such as top round, flank, or sirloin)
- 1 teaspoon *each* cornstarch, dry sherry, and soy sauce
- 1 tablespoon water
- Cooking Sauce (recipe follows)
- 2 tablespoons fermented salted black beans, rinsed, drained, and finely chopped
- 2 large cloves garlic, minced or pressed
- 1 teaspoon minced fresh ginger
- ¼ teaspoon crushed red pepper
- 1 green bell pepper, seeded and cut into 1-inch squares
- 2 green onions (including tops), cut into 1-inch lengths

Following package directions, cook noodles in boiling salted water until barely tender to bite. Drain, rinse with cold water, and drain again. Toss noodles with 1 tablespoon of the oil.

Cut beef with the grain into 1½-inch-wide strips; then cut each strip across the grain into ⅛-inch-thick slanting slices. In a bowl, stir together cornstarch, sherry, soy, and the 1 tablespoon water. Add beef and stir to coat; then stir in 1½ teaspoons of the oil. Let marinate for 15 minutes. Meanwhile, prepare Cooking Sauce and set aside.

Place a wok over high heat; when wok is hot, add 1 tablespoon of the oil. When oil begins to heat, add drained noodles and stir-fry until heated through. Remove from wok; then add remaining 1½ tablespoons oil to wok. When oil begins to heat, add black beans, garlic, ginger, and red pepper; stir once. Add beef and stir-fry for 2 minutes. Add bell pepper and onions and stir-fry for 1 more minute, adding a few drops of water if vegetables stick to wok. Stir Cooking Sauce, pour into wok, and stir until sauce boils and thickens. Return noodles to wok and toss lightly to mix. Makes 2 servings.

Cooking Sauce. Stir together ½ cup **water** and 1 tablespoon *each* **cornstarch** and **soy sauce.**

Per serving: 678 calories, 36 g protein, 52 g carbohydrates, 36 g total fat, 118 mg cholesterol, 1,185 mg sodium

(Pictured on facing page)

Bahmi Goreng

Preparation time: 15 minutes

Cooking time: 35 minutes

Indonesian *bahmi goreng* is a great way to dress up leftovers; you just combine shredded cooked meat with noodles, an assortment of vegetables, and savory seasonings. The result is always appealing and sometimes elegant enough for a party—as in this version, topped with a lattice of golden egg shreds and served with sweet-hot peanut sauce.

    Egg Shreds (recipe follows)
    Peanut Sauce (recipe follows)
2 **tablespoons soy sauce**
¼ **teaspoon anchovy paste (optional)**
4 **cups shredded cooked chicken, pork, or beef**
8 **ounces dried medium-wide noodles**
    Boiling salted water
2 **tablespoons salad oil**
4 **cloves garlic, minced or pressed**
½ **to 1 teaspoon crushed red pepper**
2 **medium-size onions, cut in half, then thinly sliced**
3 **cups thinly sliced celery**
    About ⅔ lb. cabbage, coarsely chopped
2 **cups Chinese pea pods (also called snow or sugar peas) or sugar snap peas, ends and strings removed; or 1 package (6 oz.) frozen Chinese pea pods, thawed and drained**
2 **large tomatoes, coarsely chopped**
    Salt
    Red bell pepper strips, celery leaves, cooked Chinese pea pods (optional)

Prepare Egg Shreds and Peanut Sauce; set aside.

In a bowl, stir together soy, anchovy paste (if used), and chicken; set aside. Following package directions, cook noodles in boiling salted water until barely tender to bite; drain and keep warm.

Place a wok over medium-high heat; when wok is hot, add oil. When oil is hot, add garlic, red pepper, onions, and celery. Stir-fry until vegetables are tender-crisp to bite (about 3 minutes). Add chicken mixture; reduce heat to medium and stir-fry for 3 more minutes. Add cabbage and fresh pea pods and stir-fry for 2 minutes (if using frozen pea pods, add for last 30 seconds). Add drained noodles and tomatoes and stir until heated through. Season to taste with salt. Turn onto a large platter and arrange Egg Shreds on top in a lattice design. Garnish with bell pepper strips, celery leaves, and pea pods, if desired. At the table, pass Peanut Sauce. Makes 6 servings.

Egg Shreds. Beat 2 **eggs** with a pinch of **salt.** Place a 10-inch frying pan with a nonstick finish over medium heat. When pan is hot, brush with ¼ teaspoon **salad oil.** Pour in half the beaten eggs; swirl pan to cover entire bottom. When egg sheet is lightly browned on bottom and set on top (45 seconds to 1 minute), flip it over and cook for 5 more seconds. Slide out of pan; let cool. Repeat with remaining eggs to make 1 more sheet, brushing pan with ¼ teaspoon **salad oil.** Let sheets cool; then cut in half, stack, and cut crosswise into ¼-inch-wide strips. Cover and refrigerate until ready to use or for up to 3 days.

Peanut Sauce. In a 1½-quart pan, combine 1 cup **unsweetened pineapple juice,** ⅔ cup **crunchy peanut butter,** and 2 cloves **garlic** (minced or pressed). Bring to a boil over medium heat, stirring. Remove from heat and stir in 2 tablespoons firmly packed **brown sugar,** 1 tablespoon **soy sauce,** and ¼ to ½ teaspoon **crushed red pepper.** Let cool to room temperature. If made ahead, cover and refrigerate for up to 3 days; serve at room temperature. Makes about 2 cups.

Per serving of Bahmi Goreng: 463 calories, 38 g protein, 41 g carbohydrates, 16 g total fat, 210 mg cholesterol, 996 mg sodium

Per tablespoon Peanut Sauce: 40 calories, 2 g protein, 3 g carbohydrates, 3 g total fat, 0 mg cholesterol, 54 mg sodium

Fettuccine Verde

Preparation time: About 5 minutes

Cooking time: About 5 minutes

A cream coating glistens on the spinach noodles used in this version of an Italian classic.

6 **tablespoons butter or margarine, cut in chunks**
½ **cup chopped shallots**
2 **cloves garlic, minced or pressed**
4 **cups cooked, drained spinach fettuccine**
1 **cup whipping cream**
1½ **cups grated Parmesan cheese**
¼ **teaspoon ground nutmeg**
    Salt and pepper

Place wok over medium-high heat. When wok is hot, add butter. When butter has melted, add shallots and garlic. Stir-fry until onion is limp, about 2 minutes. Add noodles and cream. Mix over high heat until cream just begins to boil. Sprinkle with 1 cup cheese; mix until noodles are well coated. Add nutmeg and salt and pepper to taste. Serve with remaining cheese. Makes 4 servings.

Per serving: 646 calories, 21 g protein, 37 g carbohydrates, 47 g total fat, 177 mg cholesterol, 759 mg sodium

Note: Recipes may be prepared in either a skillet or a wok.

As a star attraction at your next summer party, Bahmi Goreng
(recipe on facing page) will delight your guests. A lattice of tender,
golden Egg Shreds conceals a feast of marvelous flavors
from Indonesia.

Noodles with Pork & Peanut Sauce

Preparation time: About 10 minutes

Cooking time: About 10 minutes

For a quick meal, toss together hot noodles, spicy peanut sauce, mustard greens, and chunks of browned ground pork. You can brown the meat while the pasta is cooking.

        Peanut Sauce (recipe follows)
- 3 tablespoons salad oil
- 1 pound lean ground pork, pinched into 1-inch lumps

        About 4 quarts boiling salted water
- 8 ounces dried capellini or dried thin rice noodles (rice sticks)
- 4 cloves garlic, minced or pressed
- 1 medium-size onion, cut lengthwise into slender strips
- 1½ cups lightly packed slivered mustard greens

Prepare Peanut Sauce and set aside.

Place a wok over high heat; when wok is hot, add 2 tablespoons of the oil. When oil is hot, add pork. Stir-fry gently until pork is well browned (about 5 minutes).

Meanwhile, add remaining 1 tablespoon oil to about 4 quarts boiling salted water; then drop in noodles. Return to a boil; then boil, uncovered, until noodles are barely tender to bite (about 4 minutes for capellini, 2 to 4 minutes for rice noodles.) Drain.

To pork, add garlic, onion, Peanut Sauce, and 1 cup of the mustard greens; stir until boiling. Stir pork mixture into drained noodles; top with remaining ½ cup mustard greens. Makes 4 servings.

Peanut Sauce. Stir together ¼ cup *each* **soy sauce** and **regular-strength chicken or beef broth,** 2 tablespoons **creamy peanut butter,** 2 tablespoons **hoisin sauce** or tart jam, and 2 teaspoons **sugar.**

Per serving: 579 calories, 30 g protein, 57 g carbohydrates, 25 g total fat, 77 mg cholesterol, 1,477 mg sodium

Korean Bean Threads & Beef

Preparation time: About 20 minutes, plus 30 minutes to soak bean threads and mushrooms

Cooking time: 10 minutes

Here's a complete meal to cook in a wok. If you want to extend it to four servings, serve it with steamed rice and small side dishes of *kim chee*—hot, pungent pickled cabbage, available in Asian markets.

- 3 ounces dried bean threads
- 3 medium-size dried Oriental mushrooms
- 3 tablespoons sesame seeds
- ¾ pound lean boneless beef steak (such as top round, flank, or sirloin)
- 1 tablespoon sesame oil
- ¼ teaspoon black pepper
- ½ teaspoon crushed red pepper
- 2 cloves garlic, minced or pressed
- 2 tablespoons soy sauce
- 3 tablespoons salad oil
- 1 small green bell pepper, seeded and cut into thin strips
- 1 medium-size carrot, shredded
- 6 green onions (including tops), cut into 2-inch lengths
- ¼ pound bean sprouts
- ⅓ cup regular-strength beef broth
- 1 teaspoon *each* sugar and vinegar

        Salt

Soak bean threads in warm water to cover for 30 minutes. Drain, then cut into 2-inch lengths. Also soak mushrooms in warm water to cover for 30 minutes, then drain. Cut off and discard stems; squeeze caps dry and thinly slice. Set bean threads and mushrooms aside.

Place a wok over medium heat; when wok is hot, add sesame seeds and stir until golden (about 2 minutes). Pour out of wok and set aside.

Cut beef with the grain into 1½-inch-wide strips; then cut each strip across the grain into ⅛-inch-thick slanting slices. In a bowl, stir together sesame oil, black pepper, red pepper, garlic, and 1 tablespoon of the soy. Add beef and stir to coat.

Place wok over high heat. When wok is hot, add 1 tablespoon of the salad oil. When oil is hot, add beef mixture and stir-fry until meat is browned (1½ to 2 minutes); remove from wok and set aside.

Pour remaining 2 tablespoons salad oil into wok; add bell pepper, carrot, mushrooms, onions, and bean sprouts. Stir-fry for 2 minutes. Remove from wok; set aside.

Add broth, sugar, vinegar, remaining 1 tablespoon soy, and bean threads to wok. Cook, stirring frequently, until liquid is absorbed (about 2 minutes). Return meat and vegetable mixtures to wok and stir in 2 tablespoons of the sesame seeds. Season to taste with salt. Turn onto a platter and sprinkle with remaining 1 tablespoon sesame seeds. Makes 3 or 4 servings.

Per serving: 396 calories, 24 g protein, 29 g carbohydrates, 21 g total fat, 49 mg cholesterol, 646 mg sodium

Asian-style Pasta Primavera

Preparation time: About 20 minutes, plus 30 minutes to soak mushrooms

Cooking time: 30 minutes

Linguine is tossed with asparagus and favorite Asian vegetables in this light dish. You can adjust the recipe to suit available ingredients: Swiss chard can substitute for the bok choy, and button mushrooms can take the place of shiitakes.

> 3 tablespoons sesame seeds
> 8 large dried Oriental or fresh shiitake mushrooms (about 3 inches in diameter); or ½ pound fresh button mushrooms
> ½ pound *each* asparagus and bok choy
> 6 ounces dried linguine
>   Boiling salted water
> 2 tablespoons salad oil
> 2 cloves garlic, minced or pressed
> 1 tablespoon very finely chopped fresh ginger
> ½ pound Chinese pea pods (also called snow or sugar peas) or sugar snap peas, ends and strings removed; or 1 package (6 oz.) frozen Chinese pea pods, thawed and drained
> ¼ cup dry sherry
> 1 cup regular-strength chicken broth
> 2 tablespoons soy sauce
> 1 teaspoon *each* sugar and white wine vinegar

Place a wok over medium heat; when wok is hot, add sesame seeds and stir until golden (about 2 minutes). Pour out of wok and set aside.

If using dried mushrooms, soak in warm water to cover for 30 minutes, then drain. Cut off and discard stems; squeeze caps dry and thinly slice. Or trim any tough stems from fresh shiitake mushrooms; thinly slice caps. (Simply slice fresh button mushrooms thinly.)

Snap off and discard tough ends of asparagus; cut asparagus spears and bok choy stems and leaves into ½-inch slanting slices. Set vegetables aside.

Following package directions, cook linguine in boiling salted water until barely tender to bite; drain well. Place in a large, shallow serving bowl and keep warm.

Place wok over high heat; when wok is hot, add oil. When oil is hot, add garlic and ginger; stir-fry until lightly browned (about 30 seconds). Add mushrooms, asparagus, bok choy, fresh pea pods, and sherry. Cover and cook, stirring once or twice, until vegetables are bright green and tender-crisp to bite (about 2 minutes; if using frozen pea pods, add for last 30 seconds). Spoon over noodles.

Add broth, soy, sugar, and vinegar to wok; bring to a boil, stirring. Pour over noodles and vegetables. Sprinkle with sesame seeds, then mix lightly. Serve immediately. Makes 4 servings.

Per serving: 347 calories, 12 g protein, 51 g carbohydrates, 12 g total fat, 0 mg cholesterol, 806 mg sodium

(Pictured on page 95)

Italian Stir-fried Pasta

Preparation time: About 10 minutes

Cooking time: About 15 minutes

Dinner can be on the table in under half an hour when you serve this dish of *al dente* pasta mixed with onion, bell pepper, and small shrimp and topped with plenty of Parmesan cheese.

> 6 ounces dried linguine or other thin pasta
>   Boiling salted water
> 2 tablespoons olive oil
> 1 small onion, cut into bite-size pieces
> 1 medium-size green bell pepper, seeded and cut into bite-size pieces
> ¼ to ½ teaspoon crushed dried hot red chiles
> ½ to 1 teaspoon dry oregano leaves
> 1 tablespoon butter or margarine
> 2 ounces (about 18) Chinese pea pods (also called snow or sugar peas) or sugar snap peas, ends and strings removed; or ½ package (6-oz. size) frozen Chinese pea pods, thawed and drained
> ¾ pound small cooked, shelled shrimp
>   About ½ cup grated Parmesan cheese

Following package directions, cook linguine in boiling salted water until barely tender to bite; drain well and pour onto a hot platter.

While pasta is cooking, place a wok over high heat; when wok is hot, add oil. When oil is hot, add onion, bell pepper, chiles, and oregano. Stir-fry until vegetables are tender to bite (about 5 minutes).

Reduce heat to medium-high. Add butter to wok; when butter is melted, add pea pods and stir-fry for 1 minute (30 seconds if using frozen pea pods). Add shrimp, stir well, and remove wok from heat.

Spoon hot stir-fried mixture over drained pasta and serve at once. Offer cheese to sprinkle on individual servings. Makes 2 servings.

Per serving: 856 calories, 62 g protein, 72 g carbohydrates, 34 g total fat, 302 mg cholesterol, 732 mg sodium

---

Note: Recipes may be prepared in either a skillet or a wok.

Eggs, chorizo, tomatoes, tomatillos, chiles, radishes,
and cilantro contribute zest to Huevos Revueltos Rancheros
(recipe on page 77). Serve this
Southwest specialty for a hearty brunch.

Eggs

Silver Thread Stirred Eggs

Preparation time: About 10 minutes, plus 30 minutes to soak bean threads and mushrooms

Cooking time: 8 minutes

Thin, near-transparent bean threads, also sold as cellophane or shining noodles, are made from ground mung beans. They have a neutral flavor and a slippery texture; here, they add a bouncy lightness to scrambled eggs, meat, and vegetables.

- 2 ounces dried bean threads
- 4 dried Oriental mushrooms
- 2 teaspoons soy sauce
- 6 eggs
- ½ teaspoon salt
- ⅛ teaspoon white pepper
- 2 tablespoons salad oil
- 1 clove garlic, minced
- ¼ pound cooked ham, cut into match-stick pieces
- 1 stalk celery, thinly sliced
- ¼ cup sliced bamboo shoots
- 2 green onions (including tops), thinly sliced

Soak bean threads in warm water to cover for 30 minutes, then drain and cut into 4-inch lengths. Also soak mushrooms in ¾ cup warm water for 30 minutes. Remove mushrooms from water. Pour ½ cup of the soaking water into a bowl; stir in soy. Cut off and discard mushroom stems; squeeze caps dry and thinly slice. Set mushrooms and bean threads aside.

In a bowl, beat eggs with salt and white pepper; set aside.

Place a wok over high heat; when wok is hot, add oil. When oil begins to heat, add garlic and stir once; then add ham and mushrooms and stir-fry for 1 minute. Add celery and bamboo shoots and stir-fry for 2 minutes. Add bean threads and mushroom water and cook until liquid is absorbed. Add onions and cook for 30 seconds.

Reduce heat to medium. Pour eggs into wok. Cook, turning eggs occasionally with a wide spatula, until eggs are set but still soft and creamy. Makes 4 servings.

Per serving: 297 calories, 17 g protein, 17 g carbohydrates, 18 g total fat, 428 mg cholesterol, 984 mg sodium

Sausage & Greens with Eggs

Preparation time: About 15 minutes

Cooking time: About 15 minutes

Developed at a popular San Francisco restaurant, this hearty dish was originally made with spinach. Other greens taste just as good with the sausage and eggs, though; we suggest chard or kale.

- 1 pound red or green Swiss chard; or 1 pound green or red kale
- 2 tablespoons salad oil
- 1 pound mild or hot Italian sausages, casings removed
- 2 large onions, finely chopped
- 2 cloves garlic, minced or pressed
- ½ pound mushrooms, sliced
- ¼ teaspoon *each* ground nutmeg, pepper, and dry oregano leaves
- 8 eggs, lightly beaten
  Salt
- 1 cup (4 oz.) shredded jack cheese

Rinse greens well. Cut chard leaves into thin shreds; thinly slice stems. (Or cut off and discard tough stems from kale; cut leaves into thin shreds.) You should have about 8 cups, lightly packed. Set greens aside.

Place a wok over high heat; when wok is hot, add oil. When oil is hot, crumble sausage into wok; stir-fry until meat is well browned. Spoon off and discard all but 2 tablespoons of the fat. Add onions, garlic, mushrooms, nutmeg, pepper, and oregano; stir-fry until all liquid has evaporated and onions are soft. Stir in greens—a portion at a time, starting with stems—until all greens are in wok and just wilted (3 to 4 minutes). Pour eggs into wok. Stir gently over low heat just until softly set. Season to taste with salt. Transfer to a serving dish and sprinkle with cheese. Makes 4 to 6 servings.

Per serving: 522 calories, 26 g protein, 10 g carbohydrates, 42 g total fat, 439 mg cholesterol, 910 mg sodium

Note: Recipes may be prepared in either a skillet or a wok.

An Asian Brunch

The breakfast (or brunch) pancake is a universal preference. In Sri Lanka, it is made of rice flour and coconut milk, shaped like a bowl, and called a "hopper." Traditionally, the lacy-edged creation is served cradling a softly fried egg.

Authentic hoppers take their rounded shape from a small, round-bottomed pan, but you'll discover that your wok works just as well. Some of the batter is swirled around the sloping wok sides to form the crisp edges of the hopper; the remaining batter settles in the bottom, creating the pancake's thicker, slightly spongy center.

Use a well-seasoned wok brushed with salad oil or a wok with a nonstick finish. Before using a nonstick wok, it's a good idea to test it with a small amount of batter; if the batter sticks, coat the wok with a vegetable cooking spray.

Serve the warm hoppers topped with fried eggs; accompany with our Coconut Relish and Crisp Ham Ribbons. Or offer sliced tomatoes topped with chopped onions and lime, or tropical fruits such as papaya, mango, or pineapple.

Hoppers

- 1 **teaspoon active dry yeast**
- 2 **teaspoons sugar**
- 1 **cup warm water (about 110°F)**
- 1½ **cups canned or thawed frozen coconut milk**
- 1½ **cups rice flour**
  Coconut Relish (recipe follows)
  Crisp Ham Ribbons (recipe follows)
  Salad oil
- 6 **or 7 hot softly fried eggs**
  Red pepper paste or chopped fresh hot red chiles

In a large bowl, dissolve yeast and sugar in warm water. Let stand until frothy (20 to 25 minutes). Stir in coconut milk and flour until smooth. Cover and let stand at room temperature until foamy (about 2 hours) or cover and refrigerate for up to 12 hours.

Meanwhile, prepare Coconut Relish and Crisp Ham Ribbons. Set aside.

Place a wok over medium heat; when wok is hot, brush bottom and sides with oil. Pour ½ cup of the batter into center of wok all at once. Quickly tilt wok to form a thin pancake about 8 inches wide. Cover wok and cook until sides of pancake are crisp and bottom is golden (5 to 6 minutes).

With a wide spatula, loosen pancake and remove from wok; keep warm. Scrape browned bits free, grease wok, and repeat to cook remaining batter. (If you have problems with sticking, clean wok and spray with vegetable cooking spray, then heat.)

If you make pancakes ahead, place them in a single layer on baking sheets at room temperature for up to 4 hours. To reheat, set in a 350° oven, uncovered, until hot (about 5 minutes).

Serve pancakes hot, topping each with an egg. Offer Coconut Relish, Crisp Ham Ribbons, and pepper paste to add to individual servings. Makes 6 or 7 servings.

Coconut Relish. Pierce eyes of a small **coconut** and drain out liquid; discard liquid or reserve to drink as a beverage. Place coconut in a 350° oven and bake until shell begins to crack (20 to 30 minutes). Let cool. Hit coconut along crack with a hammer to break open. With a blunt knife, pry coconut meat free. Cut into about ½-inch chunks; whirl about ½ cup of the chunks in a food processor or blender to make ½ cup finely grated coconut. Reserve remaining coconut for another use. (As a substitute, you may mix ½ cup dry unsweetened shredded coconut with 2 tablespoons water.)

Mix coconut with 1 teaspoon **paprika,** ¼ teaspoon **ground red pepper** (cayenne), 2 tablespoons finely chopped **onion,** and 2 teaspoons **lime juice.** Season to taste with **salt.** If made ahead, cover and refrigerate for up to 1 day.

Crisp Ham Ribbons. Cut 6 ounces thinly sliced **cooked ham** into ¼-inch-wide strips about 3½ inches long. In a 10- to 12-inch frying pan, combine 2 tablespoons **salad oil** and ham. Stir over medium heat until ham is crisp (7 to 10 minutes). Serve warm or at room temperature.

Per serving: 458 calories, 14 g protein, 31 g carbohydrates, 31 g total fat, 260 mg cholesterol, 518 mg sodium

Herb Eggs with Yogurt Sauce

Preparation time: 15 minutes

Cooking time: About 5 minutes

It's easy to make perfect scrambled eggs in your wok! Here, the eggs are enlivened with fresh vegetables and served with a minted yogurt sauce.

Yogurt Sauce (recipe follows)
8 eggs
2 tablespoons water
¼ teaspoon pepper
1 tablespoon butter or margarine
1 tablespoon olive oil
½ cup minced parlsey
2 green onions (including tops), finely chopped
1 medium-size tomato, seeded and chopped
Salt and pepper

Prepare Yogurt Sauce and set aside. Beat eggs, water, and the ¼ teaspoon pepper until blended.

Place a wok over medium heat; when wok is hot, add butter and oil. When butter is melted, add parsley and onions and stir-fry for 1 minute. Add tomato and stir-fry for 30 seconds. Pour in eggs and stir gently until eggs are set but still moist (2 to 3 minutes). Season to taste with salt and pepper. Serve immediately with Yogurt Sauce. Makes 4 servings.

Yogurt Sauce. Stir together 1 cup **plain yogurt,** 2 tablespoons *each* minced **green onion** (including top) and **fresh mint,** 2 teaspoons **lemon juice,** and a dash of **liquid hot pepper seasoning.**

Per serving: 261 calories, 16 g protein, 8 g carbohydrates, 18 g total fat, 559 mg cholesterol, 215 mg sodium

(Pictured on page 74)

Huevos Revueltos Rancheros

Preparation time: About 10 minutes

Cooking time: 25 minutes

A treat to the eye as well as the palate, these scrambled eggs are topped with a spicy tomato-sausage sauce.

½ pound chorizo sausage, casings removed
½ cup thinly sliced green onions
1 large firm-ripe tomato, seeded and diced
½ cup diced tomatillos
1 can (4 oz.) diced green chiles
10 eggs
3 tablespoons water

2 tablespoons butter or margarine
Sliced radishes, sour cream, fresh cilantro (coriander) sprigs (optional)
Salt and pepper

Place a wok over medium heat; when wok is hot, crumble in sausage. Stir-fry until sausage is browned (about 7 minutes); spoon off and discard fat. Stir in onions, tomato, tomatillos, and chiles. Then stir occasionally until almost all liquid in sauce has evaporated and vegetables are soft (about 10 minutes). Pour into a bowl and keep warm; clean and dry wok.

Beat eggs with water until blended. Place wok over medium heat; when wok is hot, add butter. When butter is melted, pour in eggs and stir gently until eggs are set to your liking. Transfer eggs to individual plates, spoon sausage mixture over eggs; garnish with radishes, sour cream, and cilantro, if desired. Season to taste with salt and pepper. Makes 5 servings.

Per serving: 408 calories, 18 g protein, 6 g carbohydrates, 34 g total fat, 591 mg cholesterol, 632 mg sodium

Tortino Italiano

Preparation time: About 10 minutes

Cooking time: About 10 minutes

Red bell pepper and sliced zucchini add flecks of bright color to this *tortino.*

3 eggs
1 tablespoon whipping cream or water
1 tablespoon chopped parsley
1 tablespoon butter or margarine
1 tablespoon olive oil or salad oil
1 small onion, finely chopped
1 clove garlic, minced or pressed
1 medium-size zucchini, thinly sliced
1 small red bell pepper, seeded and diced
Salt and pepper
2 tablespoons grated Parmesan cheese

Beat eggs, cream, and parsley until blended.

Place a wok over medium heat. When wok is hot, add butter and oil. When butter is melted, add onion and garlic and stir-fry until onion is soft. Then add zucchini and bell pepper; stir-fry until zucchini is tender-crisp to bite (2 to 3 minutes).

Pour egg mixture over vegetables, season to taste with salt and pepper, and cook, tilting wok and poking holes between vegetables so uncooked egg flows underneath, until eggs are just set. Sprinkle with cheese; remove from heat, cover, and let stand for 1 minute. Makes 2 servings.

Per serving: 302 calories, 13 g protein, 7 g carbohydrates, 25 g total fat, 439 mg cholesterol, 262 mg sodium

Note: Recipes may be prepared in either a skillet or a wok.

Salads

(Pictured on facing page)

Hot Beef & Watercress Salad

Preparation time: About 10 minutes

Marinating time: 30 minutes

Cooking time: About 3 minutes

Hot, garlicky stir-fried beef strips top chilled watercress dressed with a light vinaigrette in this unusual salad. Marinate the meat for about half an hour before cooking or, if you like, marinate it overnight in the refrigerator.

½ pound lean boneless beef steak (such as top round, flank, or sirloin), cut about 1 inch thick
4 cloves garlic, minced or pressed
2 teaspoons soy sauce
1 teaspoon sugar
1 tablespoon salad oil
2 tablespoons white wine vinegar
¼ teaspoon pepper
1 small white onion, thinly sliced and separated into rings
About ½ pound watercress

Cut beef with the grain into 3-inch-wide strips; then cut each strip across the grain into ⅛-inch-thick slanting slices. In a bowl, stir together garlic, soy, ½ teaspoon of the sugar, and 1 teaspoon of the oil. Add beef; stir to coat. Cover and refrigerate for at least 30 minutes or until next day.

In another bowl, stir together remaining ½ teaspoon sugar, remaining 2 teaspoons oil, vinegar, and pepper. Add onion and mix lightly. Cover and refrigerate for at least 30 minutes or until next day.

Remove and discard tough watercress stems; rinse sprigs thoroughly and pat dry. Then measure 3 cups sprigs, lightly packed. Shortly before serving, add watercress to onion mixture, mixing lightly to coat. Arrange on 2 dinner plates.

Place a wok over high heat. When wok is hot, add beef mixture and stir-fry until meat is browned (1½ to 2 minutes). Arrange meat evenly atop watercress salads. Makes 2 servings.

Per serving: 258 calories, 29 g protein, 8 g carbohydrates, 12 g total fat, 65 mg cholesterol, 449 mg sodium

Hot Chicken & Fruit Salad Platter

Preparation time: 30 minutes

Cooking time: 7 minutes

Here's an extra-pretty whole-meal salad: cantaloupe chunks and warm stir-fried chicken tumbled in a sweet-sour lime sauce, then mounded atop hot rice and ringed with golden pineapple wheels.

Sweet Lime Sauce (recipe follows)
1 small cantaloupe (about 1½ lbs.)
2 whole chicken breasts (about 1 lb. *each*), skinned and boned
1 small pineapple (about 3 lbs.)
8 to 10 large romaine lettuce leaves
About 1 tablespoon salad oil
¼ cup lightly packed chopped fresh mint leaves
4 cups hot cooked rice
Fresh mint sprigs (optional)

Prepare Sweet Lime Sauce; set aside.

Seed and peel cantaloupe. Cut fruit into bite-size chunks; set aside. Cut chicken breasts across the grain into ¼-inch-thick strips; set aside.

Peel pineapple. Cut fruit crosswise into 8 equal slices; trim core from each slice, if desired. On a large platter (at least 12 inches in diameter), arrange romaine leaves with tips extending beyond rim of platter. Arrange pineapple on leaves around edge of platter. (At this point, you may cover and refrigerate sauce, cantaloupe, chicken, and salad platter separately for up to 4 hours.)

Place a wok over high heat; when wok is hot, add 1 tablespoon of the oil. When oil is hot, add half the chicken. Stir-fry until meat is no longer pink in center; cut to test (about 3 minutes). Lift out chicken with a slotted spoon and set aside. Repeat to cook remaining chicken, adding more oil as needed.

Stir sauce and pour into wok; bring to a boil, stirring. Remove wok from heat. Add chicken, cantaloupe, and chopped mint; gently turn meat and melon in sauce to coat.

Mound rice on platter atop lettuce. Spoon chicken mixture over rice; garnish with mint sprigs, if desired. Serve hot. Makes 6 servings.

Sweet Lime Sauce. Stir together ½ cup **white wine vinegar,** ¼ cup **sugar,** 1 teaspoon grated **lime peel,** 3 tablespoons **lime juice,** 2 tablespoons **soy sauce,** 1 tablespoon **cornstarch,** and ¼ teaspoon **ground red pepper** (cayenne).

Per serving: 379 calories, 21 g protein, 64 g carbohydrates, 4 g total fat, 42 mg cholesterol, 400 mg sodium

Note: Recipes may be prepared in either a skillet or a wok.

Start this extraordinary main dish by stir-frying strips of marinated beef.
Then spoon the sizzling meat over cool, crisp watercress and onions
to create Hot Beef & Watercress Salad (recipe on facing page).
Add fresh tangerines for dessert.

Hot, Wilted Salads

Usually crisp and cool, a salad takes on a completely different character when its greens are briefly touched by a hot, robustly seasoned, meaty dressing. For a light yet satisfying main dish, choose one of these six versions of the old-fashioned wilted salad. You can put each together right at the table, using an electric wok or a regular wok with a portable heat source. Or, if it's more convenient for you, you can make the salad in the kitchen, then transfer it to individual salad plates or a large salad bowl.

Wilted Romaine with Hot Sausage Dressing

Lime Dressing (recipe follows)
3 quarts bite-size pieces romaine lettuce (about 1 large head)
1 small cucumber, thinly sliced
1 large tomato, cut into wedges
1 small red onion, thinly sliced
½ cup fresh cilantro (coriander) leaves
About ⅓ pound (4 or 5) Chinese sausages (*lop cheong*), cut into ¼-inch-thick slanting slices; or ⅓ pound dry salami, thinly sliced
2 tablespoons salad oil
4 cloves garlic, minced or pressed

Prepare Lime Dressing and set aside. In a large bowl, combine lettuce, cucumber, tomato, onion, and cilantro. Set aside.

Place sausages and oil in a wok over low heat; cook, stirring occasionally, until meat is lightly browned. Add garlic and stir just until golden. Add Lime Dressing; stir just until heated through. Pour sausage mixture over lettuce mixture and toss lightly. Serve immediately. Makes 4 first-course servings, 2 entrée servings.

Lime Dressing. Stir together ⅓ cup **lime juice,** 2½ tablespoons **sugar,** 1 tablespoon **fish sauce** (*nam pla*) or soy sauce, and ½ to ¾ teaspoon **crushed red pepper.**

Per first-course serving: 299 calories, 13 g protein, 19 g carbohydrates, 20 g total fat, 0 mg cholesterol, 1126 mg sodium

Wilted Greens

¼ cup *each* salad oil and wine vinegar
2 teaspoons Dijon mustard
4 small thin-skinned potatoes, cooked, peeled, and sliced
Garlic Croutons (recipe follows)
8 slices bacon, cut into ½-inch pieces
5 cups bite-size pieces mustard or turnip greens
Salt and pepper

Stir together oil, vinegar, and mustard. Mix half the dressing with potatoes; cover and refrigerate for 2 to 4 hours. Meanwhile, prepare croutons; set aside.

Shortly before serving, place a wok over medium heat; when wok is hot, add bacon and stir-fry until crisp. While bacon is cooking, combine greens and potatoes in a salad bowl. Remove bacon from wok; add to salad. Spoon off and discard all but 3 tablespoons of the drippings; add remaining dressing to drippings and bring to a boil. Pour hot dressing over salad; invert wok over salad for a few seconds to wilt greens. Season to taste with salt and pepper; add croutons and mix well. Serve immediately. Makes 4 servings.

Garlic Croutons. In a wok or wide frying pan, combine 2 tablespoons **olive oil,** 2 cloves **garlic** (minced or pressed), and 1½ cups **French bread cubes.** Cook over medium-low to medium heat, stirring often, until bread is toasted (about 10 minutes).

Per serving: 431 calories, 8 g protein, 22 g carbohydrates, 35 g total fat, 18 mg cholesterol, 425 mg sodium

Tri-color Salami Salad

1 pound curly endive (about 2 heads)
2 tablespoons salad oil
6 ounces thinly sliced dry salami, cut into ¼-inch strips
3 tablespoons lemon juice
2 cloves garlic, minced or pressed
1 teaspoon dry basil
½ teaspoon sugar
2 cups thinly sliced cauliflowerets
2 red bell peppers, seeded and cut into ¼-inch strips

Wash endive well and shake dry, then tear into bite-size pieces. Set aside.

Place a wok over medium-high heat; when wok is hot, add oil. When oil is hot, add salami and stir-fry until edges are lightly browned. Add lemon juice, garlic, basil, and sugar; stir to blend. (At this point, you may cover mixture and let stand at room temperature for 3 to 4 hours or refrigerate until next day; transfer to another container if wok is not resistant to acid.)

Increase heat under wok to high and bring salami mixture to a boil. Add cauliflower and bell peppers and stir-fry for 1 minute. Add endive and turn off heat. Lift and turn greens and vegetables with 2 forks or spoons until endive is coated with dressing. Immediately spoon onto individual plates and serve. Makes 6 servings.

Per serving: 188 calories, 8 g protein, 7 g carbohydrates, 14 g total fat, 0 mg cholesterol, 665 mg sodium

Red Cabbage & White Sausage Salad

¼ cup salad oil
1 to 1¼ pounds white veal sausages such as bratwurst, bockwurst, or weisswurst, cut into ¼-inch slices
3 tablespoons white wine vinegar
2 tablespoons sugar
1½ teaspoons *each* Dijon mustard, celery seeds, and Worcestershire
1 clove garlic, minced or pressed
1 cup thinly sliced green onions (including tops)
6 cups finely shredded red cabbage (about 1½ lbs.)
   Salt and pepper

Place a wok over medium-high heat; when wok is hot, add oil. When oil is hot, add sausages and cook, turning frequently, until browned. Add vinegar, sugar, mustard, celery seeds, Worcestershire, and garlic. (At this point, you may let mixture stand for 3 to 4 hours at room temperature or cover and refrigerate until next day; transfer to another container if wok is not resistant to acid.)

Increase heat under wok to high and bring sausage mixture to a boil; mix in onions and cabbage.

Turn off heat; lift and turn cabbage with 2 forks or spoons until coated with dressing. Season to taste with salt and pepper; immediately spoon onto individual plates and serve. Makes 6 servings.

Per serving: 422 calories, 15 g protein, 15 g carbohydrates, 34 g total fat, 57 mg cholesterol, 592 mg sodium

Hot Spinach, Apple & Sausage Salad

1 to 1¼ pounds spinach
1¼ to 1½ pounds mild Italian sausages, casings removed
¼ cup *each* red wine vinegar and sugar
¼ teaspoon *each* ground nutmeg and dry mustard
1 large red onion, thinly sliced and separated into rings
2 large red-skinned apples, cored and thinly sliced
   Salt

Remove and discard tough spinach stems and any yellow or wilted leaves. Rinse remaining leaves well, pat dry, and set aside.

Slice or break sausages into ½-inch pieces. Place a wok over medium heat; when wok is hot, add sausages. Cook, stirring occasionally, until well browned; pour off and discard all but ¼ cup of the fat.

Add vinegar, sugar, nutmeg, and mustard to sausages and fat in wok; stir to blend. (At this point, you may let mixture stand for 3 to 4 hours at room temperature or cover and refrigerate until next day; transfer to another container if wok is not resistant to acid.)

Increase heat under wok to high and bring sausage mixture to a boil. Then add onion and apples; cook, stirring, for 1 minute. Add spinach, then turn off heat.

Lift and turn greens with 2 forks

or spoons until coated with dressing. Season to taste with salt, then serve immediately. Makes 6 servings.

Per serving: 437 calories, 19 g protein, 23 g carbohydrates, 30 g total fat, 73 mg cholesterol, 819 mg sodium

Wilted Chinese Cabbage

¼ cup sesame seeds
¼ cup salad oil
½ cup thinly sliced green onions, including tops
½ pound lean ground pork
¼ cup sugar
1 teaspoon sesame oil
6 tablespoons rice wine vinegar
1 tablespoon soy sauce
½ teaspoon pepper
1 large head napa cabbage (about 3 lbs.), finely shredded
   Fresh cilantro (coriander) sprigs

Place a wok over medium-high heat; when hot, add sesame seeds and stir-fry until golden (about 2 minutes). Pour out of wok and set aside.

Add 2 tablespoons salad oil to wok; when oil is hot, add onions and stir-fry for 1 minute. Add pork and stir-fry until meat is lightly browned (about 3 minutes).

Add remaining 2 tablespoons oil, sugar, sesame oil, vinegar, soy and pepper to wok; stir to blend. Increase heat under wok to high and bring pork mixture to a boil. Add cabbage and sesame seeds and turn off heat. Lift and turn cabbage with 2 forks or spoons until coated with dressing. Immediately spoon onto individual plates, garnish with cilantro, and serve. Makes 8 servings.

Per serving: 226 calories, 8 protein, 14 carbohydrates, 17 total fat, 21 mg cholestrol, 163 mg sodium

Note: Recipes may be prepared in either a skillet or a wok.

You'll want to linger over lunch when the main course is
Shrimp & Vegetable Salad (recipe on facing page). Soy-seasoned
broccoli, mushrooms, and delicate shrimp cascade over flavorful greens;
cashews add crunch.

Hot & Cold Ginger Chicken Salad

Preparation time: About 25 minutes

Marinating time: 30 minutes

Cooking time: About 10 minutes

Hot, gingery chicken strips contrast with cold, crisp watercress; buttery avocado slices provide a pleasant foil to the peppery flavors of meat and greens.

>   Ginger Marinade (recipe follows)
> 3 whole chicken breasts (about 1 lb. *each*), skinned, boned, and cut into ½- by 2-inch strips
> 3 tablespoons olive oil or salad oil
> ¼ cup lemon juice
> 6 cups lightly packed watercress sprigs (about 1 lb.), washed and crisped
>   Salt and pepper
> 2 large ripe avocados
> 1 lemon, cut into 6 wedges
>   About 6 tablespoons salad oil

Prepare Ginger Marinade; add chicken and mix until well coated. Let marinate at room temperature for 30 minutes, or cover and refrigerate until next day.

In a large bowl, combine olive oil and 3 tablespoons of the lemon juice; mix until well blended. Add watercress and season to taste with salt and pepper; mix lightly until well coated. Pit and peel avocados; cut lengthwise into thin wedges. Moisten with remaining 1 tablespoon lemon juice. Arrange watercress, avocado, and lemon wedges on individual dinner plates or on a platter.

Lift chicken from marinade; discard marinade. Place a wok over high heat; when wok is hot, add 2 tablespoons of the salad oil. When oil is hot, add about a third of the chicken (do not crowd wok). Stir-fry until lightly browned on outside and no longer pink in center; cut to test (about 3 minutes). Remove from wok and set aside. Repeat to cook remaining chicken, adding remaining salad oil as needed.

Spoon hot chicken over watercress and serve immediately. Makes 6 servings.

Ginger Marinade. In a large bowl, stir together 2 tablespoons **cornstarch** and ¼ cup **soy sauce** until smooth. Add ⅓ cup *each* **sesame oil** and minced **fresh ginger,** ¼ cup **lemon juice,** 1 tablespoon **salad oil,** ⅛ teaspoon **chili oil** or liquid hot pepper seasoning, and 1 clove **garlic,** minced or pressed. Mix until well blended.

Per serving: 596 calories, 44 g protein, 12 g carbohydrates, 43 g total fat, 100 mg cholesterol, 639 mg sodium

---

(Pictured on facing page)

Shrimp & Vegetable Salad

Preparation time: 20 minutes

Cooking time: 6 minutes

Chilling time: At least 4 hours

Crisp vegetables and small shrimp are chilled in a soy-flavored marinade and topped with crunchy cashews to make a satisfying one-dish lunch.

> ½ pound broccoli
> 2 tablespoons salad oil
> 2 cloves garlic, minced or pressed
> ¾ teaspoon minced fresh ginger
> ½ pound mushrooms, thinly sliced
> ½ pound Chinese pea pods (also called snow or sugar peas) or sugar snap peas, ends and strings removed; or 1 package (6 oz.) frozen Chinese pea pods, thawed and drained
> ⅓ cup regular-strength chicken broth
> 1 tablespoon soy sauce
> ½ teaspoon sugar
> 1 tablespoon oyster sauce (optional)
> 1 can (4½ oz.) small shrimp, drained
> ½ cup mayonnaise (optional)
>   Salad greens, such as butter lettuce leaves, endive spears, and dandelion greens
> ¼ cup salted roasted cashews or slivered almonds
> 1 jar (2 oz.) sliced pimentos, drained

Cut off and discard tough ends of broccoli stalks. Cut flowerets off broccoli stalks; then cut flowerets into ¼-inch-thick slices. Peel stalks and cut crosswise into ⅛-inch-thick slices. Set aside.

Place a wok over high heat; when wok is hot, add oil. When oil begins to heat, add garlic and ginger and stir-fry for 1 minute. Add broccoli, mushrooms, and fresh pea pods; stir-fry just until broccoli and pea pods are tender-crisp to bite (3 to 4 minutes; if using frozen pea pods, add for last 30 seconds). Pour into a bowl.

In a cup, stir together broth, soy, sugar, and, if desired, oyster sauce. Pour over vegetables; then stir in shrimp. Let cool, then cover and refrigerate for at least 4 hours. Drain vegetable mixture, discarding liquid. If desired, stir in mayonnaise. Spoon over greens, sprinkle with cashews, and garnish with pimentos. Makes 4 servings.

Per serving: 206 calories, 14 g protein, 14 g carbohydrates, 12 g total fat, 48 mg cholesterol, 454 mg sodium

---

Note: Recipes may be prepared in either a skillet or a wok.

Chile Shrimp & Corn Salad

Preparation time: About 20 minutes

Cooking time: 11 minutes

Chilling time: 1 to 4 hours

The salad is cold, but its flavor is *hot*: corn, bell peppers, and juicy shrimp are stir-fried in a zippy chile-infused oil. Before serving, you toss the chilled stir-fry with fresh spinach and leaf lettuce.

- ¼ cup olive oil or salad oil
- 3 small dried hot red chiles
- ½ teaspoon pepper
- 2 cups fresh corn kernels, cut from about 3 large ears of corn; or 1 package (10 oz.) frozen whole-kernel corn, thawed and drained
- 1 medium-size red bell pepper, seeded and diced
- 1 pound medium-size raw shrimp, shelled and deveined
- 1 tablespoon soy sauce
- ⅔ cup cider vinegar
- 1 pound spinach, stems and any tough or wilted leaves removed, green leaves washed and crisped
- 1 pound green leaf lettuce, washed and crisped

Place a wok over medium heat; when wok is hot, add oil. When oil is hot, add chiles and stir until lightly browned (about 4 minutes). Add pepper, corn, and bell pepper. Increase heat to high; stir-fry until bell pepper is tender to bite (about 3 minutes). Add shrimp; stir-fry just until shrimp turn pink (about 3 minutes).

Remove wok from heat. Stir in soy and vinegar, then spoon shrimp mixture into a small bowl. Let cool, then cover and refrigerate until shrimp are cold (at least 1 hour) or for up to 4 hours.

Meanwhile, tear spinach and lettuce into bite-size pieces; you should have about 4 quarts, lightly packed. Place torn greens in a large salad bowl;

spoon shrimp mixture over greens. Use chiles as garnish or remove and discard. Toss salad and serve. Makes 6 to 8 servings.

Per serving: 172 calories, 13 g protein, 14 g carbohydrates, 9 g total fat, 65 mg cholesterol, 269 mg sodium

Calamari Salad al Pesto

Preparation time: About 15 minutes

Cooking time: 7 minutes

Chilling time: At least 3 hours

Julienne strips of squid and crunchy toasted walnuts go into this delicious and attractive salad. The dressing's a homemade pesto sauce you whirl together in your blender.

- **Fresh Pesto (recipe follows)**
- ¼ cup olive oil
- 1 small onion, finely diced
- 2 cloves garlic, minced or pressed
- 3 tablespoons chopped walnuts
- 1 pound tenderized giant squid (calamari) steaks, cut into ¼-inch-wide strips
- 2 tablespoons dry sherry
- 1 medium-size red bell pepper, seeded and diced
- ¼ cup diced celery
- 1 tablespoon chopped parsley
- ¼ cup cider vinegar
- 1 tablespoon lemon or lime juice
  Salt and pepper
  About 4 cups shredded iceberg lettuce

Prepare Fresh Pesto and set aside.

Place a wok over medium heat; when wok is hot, add oil. When oil is hot, add onion, garlic, and walnuts. Stir-fry until onion is soft and walnuts are toasted (about 5 minutes). Add squid and sherry and stir-fry just until squid turns an opaque chalky white (about 1 minute); do not overcook. With a slotted spoon, transfer contents of wok to a bowl.

To squid mixture, add bell pepper, celery, parsley, Fresh Pesto, vinegar, and lemon juice; mix well. Season to taste with salt and pepper. Cover and refrigerate for at least 3 hours or until next day. Serve over lettuce. Makes 4 to 6 servings.

Fresh Pesto. In a blender or food processor, whirl until smoothly puréed ¼ cup **olive oil,** ¼ cup lightly packed **fresh basil leaves,** 2 tablespoons **pine nuts,** 1 clove **garlic,** and 1 teaspoon **dry white wine** (optional).

Per serving: 284 calories, 15 g protein, 7 g carbohydrates, 23 g total fat, 42 mg cholesterol, 67 mg sodium

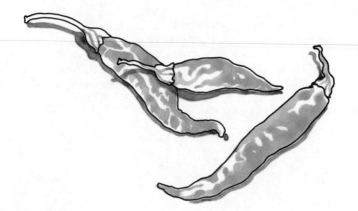

Sesame Noodle Salad

Preparation time: About 10 minutes, plus 30 minutes to soak dried mushrooms

Cooking time: 5 minutes

Chilling time: At least 2 hours

Al dente vermicelli combined with tender-crisp vegetables and a light, sweet-tart dressing makes a delightful chilled salad. For a perfect summer meal, serve it with cold roast chicken and fresh fruit in season.

> **Sesame Dressing (recipe follows)**
> 8 **medium-size fresh shiitake or dried Oriental mushrooms; or 8 large button mushrooms**
> 8 **ounces dried vermicelli**
> **Boiling salted water**
> **About 3 tablespoons salad oil**
> 2 **teaspoons minced fresh ginger**
> ¼ **pound green beans (ends removed), cut into ¼-inch slanting slices**
> 2 **medium-size carrots, peeled and cut into julienne strips**
> 2 **medium-size crookneck squash, cut into julienne strips**
> 1 **tablespoon *each* soy sauce and dry sherry**
> **Salt**

Prepare Sesame Dressing; set aside.

If using dried mushrooms, soak in warm water to cover for 30 minutes, then drain. Cut off and discard stems; squeeze caps dry. If using fresh mushrooms, trim any tough stems from shiitake mushrooms. Then set shiitake or button mushroom caps aside; cut stems into julienne strips.

Meanwhile, following package directions, cook vermicelli in boiling salted water until barely tender to bite. Drain, rinse with cold water, and drain again. Place in a large bowl and set aside.

Place a wok over high heat; when wok is hot, add 2 tablespoons of the oil. When oil is hot, add ginger, beans, carrots, squash, and julienned mushroom stems. Stir-fry just until vegetables are barely tender-crisp to bite (about 1½ minutes). Remove from wok; add to noodles.

To wok, add remaining 1 tablespoon oil, soy, sherry, and mushroom caps. Reduce heat to medium; cover wok if using dried mushrooms (leave uncovered if using fresh mushrooms). Cook, turning occasionally, until mushrooms have absorbed all liquid (about 2 minutes). Pour into a small bowl, cover, and refrigerate.

Mix dressing with noodles and vegetables. Season to taste with salt. Cover and refrigerate, stirring occasionally, for at least 2 hours or until next day.

To serve, garnish salad with mushroom caps. Makes 4 to 6 servings.

Sesame Dressing. In a wok, combine ¼ cup **salad oil** and 3 tablespoons **sesame seeds.** Stir over medium-low heat until seeds are golden (2 to 3 minutes). Remove from heat and let cool. Stir together ⅓ cup **sugar,** ½ cup **distilled white vinegar,** and 2 tablespoons **dry sherry** until sugar is dissolved. Mix in cooled sesame seed mixture.

Per serving: 402 calories, 7 g protein, 52 g carbohydrates, 19 g total fat, 0 mg cholesterol, 185 mg sodium

Soy-braised Eggplant Salad

Preparation time: 20 minutes

Cooking time: About 30 minutes

Flavored with vinegar, ginger, chiles, and soy, tender braised eggplant is equally good as an appetizer or an accompaniment to barbecued meats.

> 1 **medium-size eggplant (¾ to 1 lb.)**
> 3 **tablespoons salad oil**
> 1 **cup water**
> ¼ **cup soy sauce**
> 5 **thin, quarter-size slices fresh ginger**
> 2 **cloves garlic, minced or pressed**
> 1 **teaspoon sugar**
> 3 **tablespoons red wine vinegar**
> ⅓ **cup coarsely chopped fresh cilantro (coriander)**
> 2 **teaspoons minced fresh ginger**
> ¼ **to ½ teaspoon crushed dried hot red chiles**

Remove stem from eggplant, then peel eggplant and cut lengthwise into 1-inch-thick slices. Cut slices into 1-inch strips.

Place a wok over medium-high heat; when wok is hot, add oil. When oil is hot, add eggplant and stir-fry for 3 minutes. (Eggplant will soak up oil immediately; stir constantly to prevent burning.)

Add water, soy, ginger slices, garlic, and sugar. Reduce heat to low, cover, and simmer, stirring occasionally, until eggplant is tender when pierced (about 15 minutes). Add vinegar. Let cool, turning eggplant occasionally. (At this point, you may cover and refrigerate until next day.)

Transfer eggplant and sauce to a serving dish, then sprinkle with cilantro, minced ginger, and chiles. Serve cold or at room temperature. Makes 4 servings.

Per serving: 232 calories, 3 g protein, 11 g carbohydrates, 21 g total fat, 0 mg cholesterol, 1,035 mg sodium

---

Note: Recipes may be prepared in either a skillet or a wok.

Vegetables

Cantonese Vegetable Medley

Preparation time: About 10 minutes, plus 30 minutes to soak fungus

Cooking time: 5 minutes

Meaty "cloud ears" combine with crisp carrots, broccoli, and water chestnuts in this colorful Cantonese dish. Be sure to allow an extra half hour or so to soak the black fungus.

- ½ **cup dried black fungus (also called cloud or tree ears)**
- 1 **tablespoon** *each* **cornstarch, water, and soy sauce**
- 1 **cup regular-strength chicken broth**
- 2 **tablespoons salad oil**
- ½ **teaspoon minced fresh ginger**
- 1 **small clove garlic, minced or pressed**
- 1½ **cups** *each* **broccoli flowerets and thinly sliced carrots**
- ⅓ **cup sliced water chestnuts**

Soak fungus in warm water to cover for 30 minutes; drain. Pinch out and discard hard, knobby centers; cut remaining fungus into bite-size pieces.

In a small bowl, stir together cornstarch, water, and soy; stir in broth and set aside.

Place a wok over high heat; when wok is hot, add oil. When oil is hot, add ginger, garlic, broccoli, carrots, and fungus. Stir-fry for 1 minute. Stir cornstarch mixture; add to vegetables along with water chestnuts. Stir until sauce boils and thickens. Makes 4 to 6 servings.

Per serving: 93 calories, 2 g protein, 11 g carbohydrates, 5 g total fat, 0 mg cholesterol, 190 mg sodium

(Pictured on facing page)

Sesame-topped Vegetables

Preparation time: 10 minutes

Cooking time: 8 minutes

Malaysian *achar*, a colorful tumble of sweet-and-sour vegetables, provides a cooling contrast to any spicy entrée. Serve warm or at room temperature.

- ½ **English or European cucumber**
- 3 **large carrots**
- 3 **cups cauliflowerets**
- ½ **cup sesame seeds**
- ⅓ **cup salad oil**
- 2 **cloves garlic, minced or pressed**
- ½ **cup minced shallots**
- ½ **cup distilled white vinegar**
- ¼ **cup sugar**
    Soy sauce
    Arugula leaves (optional)

Cut cucumber and carrots into thin, about 6-inch-long slivers. Break cauliflowerets into smaller flowerets. Set vegetables aside.

Place a wok over medium heat. When wok is hot, add sesame seeds and stir until golden (2 to 3 minutes). Pour out of wok and set aside.

Pour oil into wok. When oil is hot, add garlic and shallots; stir-fry until shallots are soft. Increase heat to high and add vinegar, sugar, cauliflowerets, and carrots. Stir-fry until vegetables are tender-crisp to bite; add cucumber and stir-fry until hot. Season to taste with soy. Transfer to a serving plate; sprinkle with sesame seeds. Garnish with arugula, if desired. Makes 6 to 8 servings.

Per serving: 192 calories, 3 g protein, 17 g carbohydrates, 14 g total fat, 0 mg cholesterol, 22 mg sodium

Chinese Ginger-Garlic Asparagus

Preparation time: About 10 minutes

Cooking time: About 5 minutes

Crisp stir-fried asparagus is especially tasty when accented with garlic and fresh ginger; broccoli benefits from the same treatment.

- 1 **pound asparagus**
- 2 **tablespoons salad oil**
- 1 **large clove garlic, minced or pressed**
- ½ **to 1 teaspoon grated fresh ginger**
- 2 **tablespoons water**

Snap off and discard tough ends of asparagus, then cut spears into ¼-inch slanting slices.

Place a wok over high heat; when wok is hot, add oil. When oil begins to heat, add garlic and ginger and stir once; then add asparagus and stir-fry for 1 minute. Add water; cover and cook until asparagus is tender-crisp to bite (2 to 3 minutes). Makes 4 servings.

Per serving: 75 calories, 2 g protein, 3 g carbohydrates, 7 g total fat, 0 mg cholesterol, 1 mg sodium

Note: Recipes may be prepared in either a skillet or a wok.

Bright carrot and cucumber slivers, cauliflowerets, and sweet-sour flavorings
come together in these Sesame-topped Vegetables from Malaysia
(recipe on facing page). Garnish with arugula leaves and a delicate fan
of paper-thin cucumber slices.

Sesame-blacked Carrots

Preparation time: About 10 minutes

Cooking time: About 10 minutes

Sold in Asian markets, black sesame seeds cost and taste the same as the familiar yellow or white seeds—but they look a lot more dramatic. Here, they're toasted and blended with gingery stir-fried carrots.

- ¼ cup black sesame seeds
- 1 tablespoon olive oil or salad oil
- 1 small onion, thinly sliced
- 2 tablespoons butter or margarine
- 1½ pounds carrots (about 6 medium-size), peeled and shredded
- 1 tablespoon minced crystallized ginger
  Salt and pepper

Place a wok over medium heat; when wok is hot, add sesame seeds and stir often until seeds taste toasted and the few light-colored seeds among the black turn golden (about 2 minutes). Pour seeds out of wok and set aside.

Add oil to wok and increase heat to medium-high. When oil is hot, add onion and stir-fry until soft (about 4 minutes). Add butter, carrots, and ginger; stir-fry until carrots are tender-crisp to bite (about 3 minutes). Stir in sesame seeds and season to taste with salt and pepper. Makes 4 to 6 servings.

Per serving: 143 calories, 2 g protein, 14 g carbohydrates, 9 g total fat, 10 mg cholesterol, 77 mg sodium

Acapulco Corn Medley

Preparation time: About 15 minutes

Cooking time: About 10 minutes

Enjoy this red, green, and yellow side dish in any season—you can use either fresh or frozen corn, and the other ingredients are available year round. If you'd like to tone down the snappy flavor, cut back on the hot pepper seasoning and chili powder.

- 2 tablespoons butter or margarine
- 1 medium-size onion, chopped
- 1 red or green bell pepper, seeded and chopped
- 1 pound zucchini, cut into ½-inch cubes
- 1 canned whole green chile, seeded and chopped
- 1½ cups fresh corn kernels, cut from about 2 large ears of corn; or 1½ cups frozen whole-kernel corn, thawed and drained

- 1 can (about 14 oz.) pear-shaped tomatoes
- ¼ teaspoon liquid hot pepper seasoning
- 1 teaspoon paprika
- ½ teaspoon chili powder

Place a wok over medium heat; when wok is hot, add butter. When butter is melted, add onion and bell pepper; stir-fry until vegetables are soft (about 5 minutes).

Stir in zucchini, chile, corn, tomatoes (break up with a spoon) and their liquid, hot pepper seasoning, paprika, and chili powder. Increase heat to high; stir often until almost all liquid has evaporated and zucchini is tender to bite (about 5 minutes). Makes 4 to 6 servings.

Per serving: 102 calories, 3 g protein, 15 g carbohydrates, 7 g total fat, 10 mg cholesterol, 209 mg sodium

Szechwan Eggplant

Preparation time: About 10 minutes

Cooking time: 15 minutes

Braised in broth that's richly flavored with pork and chiles, eggplant turns out savory and tender. Use either regular eggplant or the smaller, slimmer Japanese eggplant.

- ½ cup regular-strength chicken broth
- 1 teaspoon *each* sugar and vinegar
- 1 tablespoon soy sauce
- ½ teaspoon salt
  Dash of pepper
- 1 large eggplant or about 3 Japanese eggplants (about 1¼ lbs. *total*)
- 5 tablespoons salad oil
- ¼ pound lean ground pork
- 2 green onions (including tops), finely chopped
- 1 teaspoon minced fresh ginger
- 2 teaspoons minced garlic
- 2 teaspoons hot bean sauce; or 2 small dried hot red chiles, crumbled and seeded
- 1 teaspoon cornstarch and 1 tablespoon water, stirred together
- 1 teaspoon sesame oil

In a bowl, stir together broth, sugar, vinegar, soy, salt, and pepper; set aside. Peel eggplant, if desired (don't peel Japanese eggplant); cut into strips 2 inches long and ½ inch thick.

Place a wok over medium-high heat. When wok is hot, add 3 tablespoons of the salad oil. When oil is hot, add eggplant and stir-fry for 3 minutes. (Eggplant will soak up oil immediately; stir constantly to prevent burning.) Remove from wok and set aside.

Pour remaining 2 tablespoons salad oil into wok. When oil is hot, crumble in pork and add onions, ginger, garlic, and bean sauce. Stir-fry until meat is no longer pink (about 2 minutes). Return eggplant to wok and pour in broth mixture; cover and cook over medium-low heat until eggplant is tender when pierced (about 6 minutes).

Stir cornstarch-water mixture; pour into wok and stir until sauce boils and thickens. Stir in sesame oil. Makes 4 servings.

Per serving: 264 calories, 8 g protein, 12 g carbohydrates, 22 g total fat, 19 mg cholesterol, 682 mg sodium

Quick-fried Gobo

Preparation time: 10 to 15 minutes

Cooking time: 10 minutes

Brown-skinned gobo is known in the United States as burdock—a common weed. In Japan, though, this root is a cultivated crop; its crunchy white flesh has a delicious flavor that's compatible with typical Japanese seasonings. When choosing fresh gobo in an Asian market, look for young, tender roots less than an inch in diameter.

    1   tablespoon sesame seeds
    4   cups water
    1   tablespoon vinegar
        About 1 pound gobo (also called
        burdock)
    2   tablespoons soy sauce
    2   tablespoons mirin (sweet sake) or cream
        sherry
    1   teaspoon sugar
        Few drops of liquid hot pepper
        seasoning
    2   tablespoons salad oil
        Sliced green onions (including tops)

Place a wok over medium heat; when wok is hot, add sesame seeds and stir until golden (about 2 minutes). Pour out of wok and set aside.

In a bowl, combine water and vinegar. Scrub gobo with a brush, then scrape off and discard

brown skin. Rinse well. With a small knife, slice down sides of gobo the way you'd sharpen a pencil, cutting root into shavings. Drop cut pieces immediately into vinegar-water mixture.

In a small bowl, combine soy, mirin, sugar, and hot pepper seasoning; set aside.

Return wok to medium heat. When wok is hot, add oil. When oil is hot, lift gobo from vinegar-water mixture and drain briefly; then add to wok. Stir-fry for 1 minute. Add soy mixture and stir-fry until gobo is glazed and tender-crisp to bite (5 to 6 minutes). Sprinkle with sesame seeds and onions. Makes 4 to 6 servings.

Per serving: 110 calories, 2 g protein, 13 g carbohydrates, 5 g total fat, 0 mg cholesterol, 347 mg sodium

Green Beans with Garlic

Preparation time: About 10 minutes

Cooking time: About 15 minutes

Those familiar Asian seasonings of soy, sherry, ginger, and garlic enhance just about any food; here, they accent tender-crisp green beans. Sesame seeds add extra crunch.

    4   teaspoons soy sauce
    1   teaspoon sugar
    1   tablespoon dry sherry or water
    1   tablespoon sesame seeds
    1½   tablespoons salad oil
    3   cloves garlic, minced or pressed
    1   tablespoon minced fresh ginger
    1   pound green beans (ends removed), cut
         diagonally into 2-inch lengths

In a small bowl, stir together soy, sugar, and sherry; set aside.

Place a wok over medium heat; when wok is hot, add sesame seeds and stir until golden (about 2 minutes). Pour out of wok and set aside.

Increase heat to medium-high and pour oil into wok. When oil is hot, add garlic, ginger, and beans; stir-fry for 1½ minutes. Stir in soy mixture; reduce heat to medium, cover, and cook until beans are tender-crisp to bite (4 to 7 more minutes).

Uncover, increase heat to high, and boil, stirring, until almost all liquid has evaporated (1 to 3 minutes). Pour onto a warmed platter and sprinkle with sesame seeds. Makes 4 servings.

Per serving: 105 calories, 3 g protein, 11 g carbohydrates, 6 g total fat, 0 mg cholesterol, 448 mg sodium

Note: Recipes may be prepared in either a skillet or a wok.

In all their golden glory, Sweet & Sour Carrots
(recipe on facing page) show off the Chinese cook's artistry
with humble ingredients. Covered cooking preserves
the vegetable's intense color and sweet flavor.

Broccoli with Gorgonzola & Walnuts

Preparation time: About 10 minutes

Cooking time: About 15 minutes

Gorgonzola is a creamy blue-veined cheese from a small Italian town of the same name; if you can't find the Italian product, use one of the delicious American Gorgonzolas or any other blue-veined cheese.

- 1¼ pounds broccoli
- ¼ cup butter or margarine
- ¾ cup walnut pieces
- ½ cup regular-strength chicken broth
- 1 small onion, finely chopped
- 1 teaspoon cornstarch
- 1 tablespoon white wine vinegar
- ½ teaspoon pepper
- 1 cup (about 4 oz.) crumbled Gorgonzola or other blue-veined cheese

Cut off broccoli flowerets and slash their stems; discard broccoli stalks or reserve for another use. You should have about 4½ cups flowerets.

Place a wok over medium-high heat; when wok is hot, add 1 tablespoon of the butter. When butter is melted, add walnuts and stir-fry until browned (about 1½ minutes). Transfer to a bowl; set aside.

Wipe wok clean and add 2 tablespoons more butter; when butter is melted, add broccoli and stir-fry for 3 minutes. Add ¼ cup of the broth, cover, and cook until tender-crisp to bite (about 5 more minutes). Transfer broccoli to bowl with walnuts.

Wipe wok clean again and add remaining 1 tablespoon butter; when butter is melted, add onion and stir-fry until golden brown (about 3 minutes). Mix cornstarch with remaining ¼ cup broth, add to wok, bring to a boil, and boil for 30 seconds. Reduce heat to low; stir in vinegar, pepper, broccoli, and walnuts and cook until heated through (about 2 minutes). Add cheese and stir until partially melted. Makes 2 or 3 servings.

Per serving: 536 calories, 20 g protein, 20 g carbohydrates, 46 g total fat, 70 mg cholesterol, 901 mg sodium

Spicy Napa Cabbage

Preparation time: About 5 minutes

Cooking time: 4 minutes

Spiced with ground red pepper, mild-flavored napa cabbage turns zesty—and makes a good companion dish for roast pork or ham.

- 2 tablespoons white wine vinegar
- 2 tablespoons sugar
- 1 tablespoon soy sauce
- ¼ teaspoon ground red pepper (cayenne)
- 3 tablespoons salad oil
- 1 small head napa cabbage (1¼ to 1½ lbs.), cut into 2-inch pieces

In a small bowl, stir together vinegar, sugar, soy, and red pepper; set aside.

Place a wok over high heat; when wok is hot, add oil. When oil is hot, add cabbage and stir-fry until cabbage begins to wilt (2 to 3 minutes). Add vinegar mixture and mix well. Serve warm or at room temperature. Makes 4 to 6 servings.

Per serving: 137 calories, 2 g protein, 11 g carbohydrates, 10 g total fat, 0 mg cholesterol, 362 mg sodium

(Pictured on facing page)

Sweet & Sour Carrots

Preparation time: About 10 minutes

Cooking time: 8 minutes

A simple, not-too-sweet sauce intensifies the natural sweetness of carrots. The sauce enhances cauliflower and green beans, too.

- ¼ cup regular-strength chicken broth
- 2 tablespoons *each* vinegar and firmly packed brown sugar
- 1 tablespoon cornstarch
- 1 tablespoon salad oil
- 1 pound carrots (about 4 medium-size), cut into ¼-inch-thick slanting slices
- 1 small onion, cut in half, then cut crosswise into ¼-inch-thick slices
- 3 tablespoons regular-strength chicken broth
- Salt
- Minced parsley (optional)

In a bowl, stir together the ¼ cup broth, vinegar, sugar, and cornstarch. Set aside.

Place a wok over high heat; when wok is hot, add oil. When oil is hot, add carrots and onion and stir-fry for 1 minute. Add the 3 tablespoons broth and reduce heat to medium; cover and cook until carrots are tender-crisp to bite. Increase heat to high. Stir cornstarch mixture, pour into wok, and stir until sauce boils and thickens. Season to taste with salt. Sprinkle with parsley, if desired. Makes 4 servings.

Per serving: 114 calories, 1 g protein, 20 g carbohydrates, 4 g total fat, 0 mg cholesterol, 147 mg sodium

Note: Recipes may be prepared in either a skillet or a wok.

Hominy Fry Delight

Preparation time: About 10 minutes

Cooking time: 4 minutes

Plump grains of white or yellow hominy look like tiny dumplings among the vegetables in this dish. Lemon pepper adds a pleasantly tangy accent.

> 2 tablespoons salad oil
> 1 medium-size carrot, thinly sliced
> 1 medium-size red or green bell pepper, seeded and cut into thin, short strips
> 1 medium-size zucchini, thinly sliced
> 1 can (about 1 lb.) white or yellow hominy, drained
> ½ teaspoon lemon pepper
> 3 green onions (including tops), sliced
> 1 tablespoon Worcestershire

Place a wok over high heat; when wok is hot, add oil. When oil is hot, add carrot, bell pepper, zucchini, hominy, and lemon pepper. Stir-fry until vegetables are tender-crisp to bite (about 3 minutes). Stir in onions and Worcestershire; serve. Makes about 4 servings.

Per serving: 148 calories, 2 g protein, 20 g carbohydrates, 7 g total fat, 0 mg cholesterol, 467 mg sodium

Parsnip & Carrot Sauté with Tarragon

Preparation time: About 10 minutes

Cooking time: About 5 minutes

A sprinkling of tarragon is a perfect accent for sweet, tender carrots and parsnips in this easy side dish.

> 3 *each* medium-size parsnips and carrots (about 1½ lbs. *total*)
> 5 tablespoons butter or margarine
> 1 tablespoon minced shallot or onion
> ⅓ cup regular-strength chicken broth
> 1 tablespoon fresh tarragon leaves, chopped, or 1½ teaspoons dry tarragon
> 2 tablespoons minced parsley

Peel parsnips and carrots and cut into matchstick pieces. Set aside.

Place a wok over medium-high heat; when wok is hot, add butter. When butter is melted, add shallot and stir once. Add carrots and parsnips; stir-fry just until tender-crisp to bite (about 2 minutes). Add broth, cover, and cook until tender to bite (2 to 3

more minutes). Stir in tarragon and parsley; serve. Makes 4 servings.

Per serving: 223 calories, 2 g protein, 22 g carbohydrates, 15 g total fat, 39 mg cholesterol, 262 mg sodium

(Pictured on page 2)

Zucchini Sticks

Preparation time: About 10 minutes

Cooking time: 4 minutes

For a simple side dish that's also light on calories, cut zucchini into strips, then stir-fry in a bit of oil. Season simply with garlic and pepper—or add a sprinkle of Parmesan cheese.

> 4 medium-size zucchini (about 1½ lbs. *total*)
> 1 tablespoon olive oil or salad oil
> 2 cloves garlic, minced or pressed
> Pepper
> Enoki mushrooms and red bell pepper (optional)
> Grated Parmesan cheese (optional)

Cut zucchini in half lengthwise. Then cut each half lengthwise into thirds.

Place a wok over medium heat; when wok is hot, add oil. When oil is hot, add zucchini and garlic and stir-fry gently until zucchini is tender-crisp to bite (about 3 minutes). Season to taste with pepper and serve immediately. If desired, garnish with mushrooms and bell pepper and offer cheese to sprinkle atop individual servings. Makes 4 servings.

Per serving: 61 calories, 2 g protein, 7 g carbohydrates, 4 g total fat, 0 mg cholesterol, 2 mg sodium

Matchstick Zucchini with Marinara Sauce

Place a wok over medium-high heat; when hot, add 2 tablespoons **olive oil.** When oil is hot, add 1 clove **garlic,** minced or pressed, and 1 **onion,** finely chopped; stir-fry until golden (about 3 minutes). Add ¼ cup **fresh basil leaves,** finely chopped, and 1½ pounds **tomatoes,** peeled, cored, and finely chopped. Cook, stirring occasionally, for 15 minutes. Add ½ teaspoon **sugar** and season to taste with **salt** and **pepper.** Keep warm while preparing zucchini. Follow directions for **Zucchini Sticks,** but cut zucchini lengthwise into thin slices; then cut slices into 4 or 5-inch long julienne strips and reduce cooking time to 2 minutes. Omit mushrooms and red bell pepper; serve with sauce and cheese.

Greens & Tofu in Peanut Sauce

Preparation time: 10 minutes

Cooking time: 15 minutes

Tofu, cabbage, spinach, and bean sprouts dressed with a delicious peanut-coconut sauce are served over rice noodles in this Thai specialty. If you like, top servings with crisp onion flakes; they're sold in Asian grocery stores.

- ⅓ cup crunchy peanut butter
- 1 small can (7¾ oz.) sweetened coconut milk
- 2 cloves garlic, minced or pressed
- 1½ tablespoons *each* white vinegar and soy sauce
- 1 teaspoon grated fresh ginger or ¼ teaspoon ground ginger
- ⅛ to ¼ teaspoon ground red pepper (cayenne)
- 1 tablespoon peanut oil or salad oil
- 2 cups *each* thinly shredded cabbage and spinach
- ½ cup thinly sliced green onions (including tops)
- 2 cups bean sprouts
- ½ pound firm tofu (bean curd), cut into ½-inch cubes
- 8 ounces dried thin rice noodles (rice sticks) or Chinese wheat flour noodles, cooked; or 4 to 5 cups hot cooked rice
- ½ cup crisp onion flakes (optional)

In a small pan, combine peanut butter, coconut milk, garlic, vinegar, and soy. Stir over medium heat until well combined; then continue to cook, uncovered, for 3 minutes. Remove from heat and stir in ginger and red pepper.

Place a wok over medium heat; when wok is hot, add oil. When oil is hot, add cabbage and spinach and stir-fry until greens are slightly wilted (about 2 minutes). Stir in onions and bean sprouts, then add tofu and peanut sauce; stir gently to mix well. Cover and cook just until heated through.

Serve over noodles and, if desired, sprinkle with onion flakes. Makes 4 to 6 servings.

Note: To cook rice noodles, in a 5- to 6-quart pan, bring 4 quarts of salted water to a boil. Add noodles and return to a boil; then boil, uncovered, until noodles are barely tender to bite (2 to 4 minutes). Drain; rinse with hot water, drain again, and serve immediately.

Per serving: 366 calories, 12 g protein, 40 g carbohydrates, 19 g total fat, 0 mg cholesterol, 348 mg sodium

Tofu & Vegetable Stir-fry

Preparation time: about 15 minutes

Cooking time: 6 minutes

For a speedy vegetarian meal, try Vietnamese *rau xao*. The dish is made in countless variations; this one features vegetables readily available in North American markets.

- ½ pound medium-firm tofu (bean curd), cut into ½-inch cubes
- 3 tablespoons soy sauce
- 1 teaspoon rice wine vinegar or white vinegar
- ¼ teaspoon ground cumin
- 2 cloves garlic, minced or pressed
- ½ teaspoon grated fresh ginger or ⅛ teaspoon ground ginger
- 3 tablespoons peanut oil or salad oil
- 1 large carrot, chopped
- 2 cups thinly sliced broccoli stems and bite-size flowerets
- 1 cup *each* bean sprouts and sliced mushrooms
- ½ cup thinly sliced green onions (including tops)
- 3 tablespoons minced fresh cilantro (coriander)

Place tofu in a shallow bowl. In another bowl, mix soy, vinegar, cumin, garlic, and ginger; drizzle over tofu. Set aside.

Place a wok over high heat. When wok is hot, add oil. When oil is hot, add carrot and stir-fry for 1 minute; add broccoli and stir-fry for 2 more minutes. Then mix in bean sprouts, mushrooms, and onions; stir-fry for 30 more seconds.

Reduce heat to medium-high. Add tofu mixture and stir gently just until tofu is heated through but vegetables are still crisp (1 to 2 minutes). Garnish with cilantro. Makes 4 servings.

Per serving: 181 calories, 7 g protein, 11 g carbohydrates, 13 g total fat, 0 mg cholesterol, 800 mg sodium

Note: Recipes may be prepared in either a skillet or a wok.

Desserts

Apple-Blueberry Delight

Preparation time: About 10 minutes

Cooking time: About 10 minutes

Use crisp, tart apples for this sweet and spicy dessert. For a special treat, cover the hot fruit with cold whipped cream before serving.

- 2 **tablespoons sugar**
- 1 **teaspoon ground cinnamon**
- ¼ **teaspoon ground nutmeg**
  Juice and grated peel of 2 large oranges
- 4 **tart green-skinned apples (such as Granny Smith)**
- 2 **tablespoons butter or margarine**
- 1 **tablespoon orange-flavored liqueur**
- 1 **pint blueberries**
  Whipped cream (optional)

In a small bowl, mix sugar, cinnamon, and nutmeg; set aside.

In a large bowl, mix orange juice and peel. Peel, core, and thinly slice apples; toss with juice.

Place a wok over medium heat; when wok is hot, add butter. When butter is melted, add sugar mixture and cook, stirring constantly, for about 1 minute.

Add apple mixture to wok and stir-fry until apples are soft (about 3 minutes). Add liqueur, bring to a boil, and boil for about 1 minute. Add blueberries and stir-fry until sauce is thickened. Serve hot, topped with whipped cream, if desired. Makes 4 to 6 servings.

Per serving: 157 calories, 1 g protein, 35 g carbohydrates, 5 g total fat, 10 mg cholesterol, 43 mg sodium

Bananas Managua

Preparation time: About 10 minutes

Cooking time: 6 minutes

Here's a tropical delicacy that's decidedly elegant, yet quick and easy to prepare. If you'd like to top it with homemade Mexican Cream, be sure to start a few days ahead; the cream needs plenty of time to thicken and develop its tangy flavor.

- ¾ **cup sour cream or Mexican Cream (recipe follows)**
- 3 **large firm-ripe bananas**
- ⅓ **cup orange juice**
- 6 **tablespoons firmly packed brown sugar**
- 1 **teaspoon ground cinnamon**
- 3 **tablespoons butter or margarine**
- 2 **tablespoons lime or lemon juice**

If using Mexican Cream, prepare 2 days ahead.

Peel bananas and cut into ¼-inch-thick slanting slices. Pour orange juice into a small, shallow bowl. Mix sugar and cinnamon in another bowl.

Place a wok over medium heat; when wok is hot, add 1 tablespoon of the butter. When butter is melted, dip a third of the banana slices into orange juice and then into sugar mixture. Add to wok and cook until lightly browned and glazed on both sides (about 1 minute). Spoon into 2 shallow dessert dishes. Repeat with remaining bananas, using remaining 2 tablespoons butter and filling 4 more dessert dishes.

When all bananas have been cooked, add lime juice and any remaining orange juice and sugar mixture to wok. Cook over medium heat, stirring, until mixture boils and becomes syrupy (this happens quickly). Pour evenly over bananas. Top each serving with a dollop of sour cream or Mexican Cream. Serve immediately. Makes 6 servings.

Mexican Cream. In a small pan, warm 1 cup **whipping cream** to between 90° and 100°F; add 1 tablespoon **buttermilk** or sour cream, mixing well. Cover and let stand at room temperature (68° to 72°F—or put in a yogurt maker) until mixture starts to thicken (12 to 16 hours).

Refrigerate for at least 24 hours before using to allow acid flavor to develop and cream to thicken further; cream should be of almost spreadable consistency. Store in refrigerator for up to 2 weeks or as long as taste is tangy but fresh. Makes 1 cup.

Per serving: 258 calories, 2 g protein, 32 g carbohydrates, 15 g total fat, 49 mg cholesterol, 77 mg sodium

Note: Recipes may be prepared in either a skillet or a wok.

Index

*A magnificent meal, Italian Stir-fried Pasta
(recipe on page 73) combines Italian cuisine with
Oriental cooking techniques.*